Preface

——

In this world nothing can be said to be certain, except death and taxes.

BENJAMIN FRANKLIN

When Ben Franklin penned those words, he was eighty-three and, as it turned out, only five months from death. In that same letter he wrote, "I grow thinner and weaker, so that I cannot expect to hold out much longer." But considering that men in Franklin's day lived only thirty-six years on average, he had already beaten the odds by a long shot.

I have always been consumed with planning. Even as a little boy, I could not go to sleep at night until my mom tucked me in by reviewing our schedule for the next few days—no bedtime stories for me. I wanted a planning session. It's no wonder I grew up to become an estate-planning attorney and have written a book about how to plan. Not everyone is as consumed with planning as I am, I know, but almost everyone I've met likes the feeling that comes with having a plan. I did not write this book to convince you that planning is important. If you don't already know you need a plan, this may not be the book for you. If you agree with Ben Franklin, that "by failing to prepare, you are preparing to fail," but you just don't know where to start, you need this book.

So where *do* you start? Like Franklin, I believe we should begin with those things that are certain in life—death and taxes. Whether you are the parent of young children in need of protection, a member of the growing sandwich generation struggling to raise teenagers while caring for aging parents, a boomer eyeing retirement, or one of the record number of eighty- and ninety-year-olds in the United States, you would be naive to ignore what could happen when you no longer are around. And unless you believe Congress will soon do away with most of the Internal Revenue Code, I don't think I have to convince you of the importance of tax planning. Your estate plan should center on these certainties of life.

Today one more area of planning is almost as important as

death and taxes—long-term care. Planning for long-term care was irrelevant in Franklin's day when life expectancy was only thirty-six years. But Americans' life expectancy has now reached a record high of about eighty years, and those who reach the age of sixty-five are expected to live to eighty-five or beyond. This is great news...so long as you plan for these extra years.

Seventy percent of people older than sixty-five will need long-term care. That's a staggering percentage. I hope this isn't a news flash: long-term care is expensive. The best plan in the world is worth little if you have nothing left when you're gone or, worse, if you run out of money before you die. For this reason, I believe planning for long-term care is just as essential as planning for death and taxes.

Like I said, even as a kid, I couldn't relax until I had a plan, and I don't think I'm alone in feeling that way. I can't tell you how many clients shake my hand or give me a hug as they leave my office because they are relieved to know they finally are prepared for whatever life might send their way. Not everyone has the same plan, or the same motivation for planning, but the sense of confidence and well-being that comes with planning seems to be universal.

You need a plan. Let me show you how to prepare for death, taxes, and long-term care.

Introduction

My grandparents' story is a classic example of the planning errors and missed opportunities that I see every day in my law practice. In fact, the stress they experienced and the money they wasted were the inspiration for this book.

My grandparents knew they needed a plan; that wasn't the problem. This is not a story of a family that failed to plan and suffered the consequences. My grandparents made the wise decision to execute a trust years before they died. But their children had to take their estate through probate court anyway, because my grandparents didn't use the trust properly. Also, they could have received veterans' benefits to help pay for long-term care—benefits that would have eased their minds and protected the assets they had worked all their lives to accumulate. But they never received any benefits to which they were entitled because they never applied. We didn't know about them.

But I'm getting ahead of myself. Let me introduce you to Elbert and Florene Elrod.

My grandfather was born in 1913 in a shotgun-style house in Grant County, Arkansas. At an early age, he learned to hunt deer and squirrel on family land, and he continued to hunt deer in those woods as long as my grandmother would let him. On the wall of my office hang two sets of antlers: one dated 1927 and the other 1995; they are my grandfather's first and last deer.

Like many proud Americans, my grandfather volunteered for the army a couple of months after Pearl Harbor. He was twenty-seven when he entered the service, and he was stationed in Alaska's Aleutian Islands. His only complaint, at least the only complaint I ever heard him make, was how hard it was to shave with cold water...*really* cold water.

He met Florene in 1941, just before he shipped out, and they married after his discharge in 1944. My grandfather was thirty-one when they married, but my grandmother was only twenty-two. She had been a high school basketball standout back before women played the full-court game, and she traveled with a women's singing quartet that even got a little airtime on the radio.

From the time my grandfather returned from the war until the day he retired, he worked for only one company—Arkansas Power & Light, or "the power company," as he called it. He elected early retirement at sixty-two because he had seen several friends die within months of retirement; he wanted to retire early enough to enjoy life for a little while. As it turned out, he lived to be ninety, so he spent almost one-third of his life in retirement. We should all be so lucky.

My grandmother was an entrepreneur. She sold everything from Shaklee Vitamins to exercise trampolines to Amway, and she was self-employed as a beautician for most of her life. My grandfather built a beauty shop right off the side of their house, so she was able to work from home. My grandfather and I were probably my grandmother's last customers; she cut our hair until she could no longer hold scissors because of the arthritis in her hands. While she was working full time, she also cooked three full meals every day, usually meat from deer camp and vegetables from my grandfather's garden. They were way ahead of the organic movement.

My grandfather never earned more than $20,000 a year, but he never had a debt in his life. Despite their modest means, my grandparents left their children a house worth about $70,000 that my grandfather had mostly built by hand, a rental house also worth about $70,000 (they had bought it and lived there a few years because they liked the school district), and other assets totaling about $70,000. Looking back, it's hard to figure how they lived in retirement for so long on such a low income and still left so much to their children.

Speaking of children, my grandparents had three, each born ten years apart. Elbert and Florene were devoted parents who raised their kids in a Christian home. They were in church every time the doors were open. My grandfather was a greeter at church right up until he couldn't stand long enough to do the job, and then he sat on a stool by the door so he could continue just a little while longer.

My grandfather worked a huge vegetable garden all his life. It provided more than enough for my grandmother's kitchen, and they gave away food to anyone who needed it. My grandfather also mowed his own yard even into his eighties. In fact, his desire to mow sent him to a doctor for the first time since his army physical. He complained about his lack of energy, so the doctor ordered tests, and the results prompted emergency bypass surgery. The situation must have been bad—the doctor kept my grandfather in the hospital from the moment the test results came in until he was on the operating table. My grandfather later declared the entire ordeal to be a complete waste of time, because even with the surgery, he still couldn't mow his entire yard in one day.

About three years later, my grandparents began to need a lot of help in order to stay in their home. Before long, someone in the family was going to their house almost every day to bring food, help with medicine, keep up the house, and take care of the yard. If you want to know the truth, my grandfather would have been happy without food and medicine, so long as someone mowed that yard. The regular visits continued right up until my grandfather died at the age of ninety.

My grandmother, older than eighty by this time, could not remain in the house by herself, so she moved in with my aunt and her young family. My dad and his siblings could have been the poster children for the sandwich generation. My dad had two boys who were in junior high when my grandparents began to need help at home, and my aunt still had kids in elementary school when my grandmother moved in with her. Don't misunderstand: no one complained for a second, but you know it wasn't easy.

After living with my aunt for about a year, my grandmother made the move to assisted living. She probably would have done it sooner, but she constantly worried about money, and she couldn't comprehend spending so much for an apartment and meals that were nowhere near as good as what she had prepared. In fact, my grandparents might have moved to assisted living together years earlier had they not worried about money. My dad once talked to my grandfather about a new assisted living facility nearby. But when my grandfather asked how much it cost, my dad estimated that it would be about $3,000. My grandfather almost fell out of his chair and declared, "There's no way we can afford $3,000 a year!" Of course, my dad meant $3,000 a month. It is a shame that they never knew about the veterans' benefits that my grandfather had earned, which would have paid for a big percentage of these costs.

When my incredibly social grandmother moved into assisted living, she loved it. Unfortunately, she was able to remain in assisted living for only about a year. She suffered a stroke that left her with limited mobility and the inability to speak. Although she spent time in rehabilitation, she never recovered enough to return to assisted living. She spent the last year of her life in a nursing home before dying about three years after my grandfather. With a little planning, my grandmother could have qualified for Medicaid, which would have covered much of her monthly nursing home bill and protected my grandparents' hard-earned assets. Because she never planned for or applied for Medicaid benefits, she was forced to liquidate assets at an alarming rate to pay for her nursing home care.

When he was trying to settle my grandparents' estate, my dad stumbled upon papers showing they had set up a trust. It never occurred to him that they might have known what a trust was, much less that they had spent the money to create one. His surprise turned to disappointment, however, when he found that my grandparents never put any of their assets in the name of their trust. In other words, they never funded the trust. A trust is a great tool for keeping an estate out of probate, but it works only when assets have been titled in the name of the trust or properly set up to pass to the trust at death. It's still frustrating to think about how my grandparents must have struggled with the decision to pay a lawyer to set up a trust and probably felt a sense of pride that they had gotten their affairs in order. But because the trust was never funded, my dad had to put their estate through probate court.

My grandparents' story highlights a prevalent problem in the field of estate planning. I am sure the lawyer they hired to prepare their trust did exactly what they asked him to do—he prepared a trust. He obviously didn't talk to them about the availability of veterans' benefits or other planning options for long-term care. He didn't even help them fund the trust. But my grandparents and their estate-planning attorney made a mistake that I see people make all the time. They focused on only one aspect of estate planning and ignored all others. The result was a weak plan that failed to protect them and their family.

To create a strong estate plan, you must consider three distinct strands of planning. To be ready for those things in life that are certain (or almost certain), you must prepare for death, taxes, and long-term care. With that mind, this book is divided into three parts.

Part 1 focuses on death—or, more accurately, on the methods available to transfer your estate to your heirs after you die. In chapter 1, I explain how not to do it—through probate court. Chapter 2 outlines several methods for staying out of probate court and simplifies the often misunderstood world of trusts. Chapter 3 discusses some details that many planners overlook and covers planning options you probably never realized were available to you to protect your heirs.

Part 2 focuses on taxes, particularly how to minimize them. Chapter 4 discusses why estate and gift taxes are a red herring: most families do not need to worry about them. Chapter 5 zeroes in on an often overlooked but more important area of concern in estate planning: capital gains taxes. And in chapter 6, I discuss the problem caused by

IRAs (individual retirement accounts) in estate planning and how to avoid it.

Part 3 dives into the murky waters of long-term care. Chapter 7 is an overview of the four ways to pay for it. In chapter 8, I teach you why planning before you need long-term care is the safest option for assuring you can pay for it without liquidating everything you have. And in chapter 9, I show you how to qualify for assistance in paying for long-term care, even at the eleventh hour when advance planning is no longer an option.

The most challenging thing about these three strands of planning is the degree to which they intertwine. Focusing on any one strand to the exclusion of the others can be disastrous. For example, you saw how my grandparents focused exclusively on avoiding probate (and didn't succeed at that) while totally ignoring the need to plan for long-term care. This narrow focus caused them to miss out on veterans' benefits and Medicaid, created unnecessary stress for them and their children, and wasted money. At least their mistakes didn't lead to extra taxes. One of the least expensive ways to avoid probate is to sign over property using a quitclaim deed. But people who do this to save money are unaware of the high capital gains taxes their heirs may face as a result. That's why it's not a good idea to look at each strand in isolation or, worse, focus on only one strand and ignore the others. You end up with bigger problems than the ones you solve.

If you think about it, estate plans are like ropes. For thousands of years, people have known that three strands are stronger than one. In the epic of Gilgamesh, the oldest surviving work of literature ever discovered, the author made just that point when he boldly claimed that "no man can snap the triple cord," referring to the almost unbreakable three-stranded rope in common use more than four thousand years ago. This wisdom is repeated in Ecclesiastes, which teaches, "Though one may be overpowered, two can defend themselves. A cord of three strands is not quickly broken." Whether you want a strong rope or a strong estate plan, you need three strands.

The first strand of planning, which I discuss in part 1, focuses on how your estate passes to the next generation—most important, how to avoid probate. Lots of people have fallen into the probate trap, just like my grandparents did, but it proved much more costly to the families of Jimi Hendrix and Elvis Presley than to my family. By the time you finish part 1, you'll have a strong understanding of what probate is, why you want to avoid it, and the best ways to do just that.

PART I

The First Strand: The Method of Transfer

(Or How Things Get Where You Want Them to Go)

CHAPTER ONE

Probate: A Process Worth Avoiding

—

Elvis Presley may have been the king, but he certainly wasn't treated like royalty when his estate was passing through probate court in Tennessee.

Elvis had an estimated $10 million estate when he died in 1977, but after attorney fees, executor fees, taxes, court costs, and appraisal costs, only about $3 million was left for his daughter. Elvis had a last will and testament, but a will does not keep an estate out of probate. Elvis's failure to plan to avoid probate court cost his daughter $7 million.

Then there's Jimi Hendrix, who was only twenty-seven when he died in 1970. At least Elvis had a will to ensure his estate went to the right person—what was left of it, anyway. Hendrix did not have a will. He did not have a trust. He left no instructions at all, which caused more trouble than he could have imagined.

Because he was so young, his estate was not large when he died, although he was already known as an amazing musician. Jim Hendrix's father, Al Hendrix, inherited his son's estate although the two were not close; in fact, Jimi had bounced from foster home to foster home for most of his childhood. Many people who knew Jimi Hendrix believe he would have left everything to his half brother, Leon, the only person the musician really considered family. But because he died without an estate plan, his estate went to his next of kin as defined by state law, even though his closest living relative was an absentee father. And the rights to Jimi's music and his likeness proved to be extremely valuable.

All states have rules for handling the probates of the estates of people who leave no formal, written instructions, but in many cases, those rules do not match the wishes of the deceased. Just ask Jimi Hendrix.

His lack of planning resulted in several extended lawsuits about who would inherit his estate. After Al Hendrix won, he managed the estate for about twenty years. When he died in 2002, his will left control and ownership of his son's estate, then worth $80 million, to Al's adopted daughter, Janie, cutting Leon out entirely. Jimi barely knew Janie. Al's decision to cut Leon out then led to a whole new line of lawsuits more than two decades after Jimi died.

It was an especially ugly battle. According to a 2007 story in the *Seattle Times*, the case was "rife with allegations of illegitimacy, drug abuse, greed and adultery—Leon Hendrix's lawyers claimed Janie Hendrix schemed and took advantage of their father's poor health and legal naiveté to have Leon cut from the will. Janie's lawyers countered that Al cut off his younger son after he grew tired of Leon's drug addictions, chronic requests for money and refusals to work."

The Washington State Supreme Court upheld Al's will in 2007, but that did not end the family strife. In 2009, Janie Hendrix and what had become her company, Experience Hendrix, sued Leon and his business partner, alleging trademark infringement in connection with Jimi-related merchandise they were selling. That suit continued until August 2015, when the parties reached an out-of-court settlement for terms that were not disclosed.

Creating a strong estate plan begins with making sure your

estate goes where you want it to go, in the way you want it to get there, without going through probate court. But that's only the first of the three distinct strands of planning that make up a strong estate plan. The second strand involves tax considerations you must keep in mind when developing your plan; I will take up the second strand in part 2. The third strand considers the high cost of long-term care and how to pay for it, which I address in part 3. Here, in part 1, I will teach you the best ways to stay out of probate court.

It's easy to get caught up in stories like those of Elvis and Jimi Hendrix and think, "That sort of thing only happens to celebrities. Those warnings don't apply to people like me." If that's what you're thinking, you're wrong. Even middle-class Americans, folks who feel like they don't have much, can wind up in a mess when they don't plan. I recently wrapped up a probate that had gone on for years. When my client first approached me, he primarily wanted to ensure he would be eligible for veterans' benefits if he needed them to pay for long-term care. He had a will but no trust, and information he'd read about the aid and attendance benefits available through the U.S. Department of Veterans Affairs (VA) convinced him to look into doing more planning. Unfortunately, he died before we had a chance to prepare and execute his new plan.

He didn't have a large estate—just a house, a modest bank account, and two parcels of forty acres each. He wanted to put his house and land into a type of trust that would allow his estate to avoid probate while also making him eligible for veterans' benefits, but because he died before making the transfers, we had to take his estate through what I assumed would be a short and simple probate.

Three years and many headaches later, we finally closed the estate. This client had five daughters, and one decided she wasn't being treated fairly, even though the will divided the estate equally among the sisters, which is exactly what the executor set out to do. Selling the house took a while, dividing the personal property caused some hurt feelings, and small issues along the way made things more difficult than they should have been, so this unhappy daughter hired her own attorney. Every beneficiary of an estate has a right to his or her own attorney, but usually one attorney handles the entire matter for the whole family. Because she hired her own attorney and challenged everything the executor did, this probate wound up costing the daughters much more than if it had been uncontested. The result was a three-year probate for a modest estate.

These weren't celebrities. This is a true story of a real family that will never heal the rifts caused by the probate process. Not every probate story is as bad; many probates are uncontested. But because the probate process is an invitation to fight, estates that must pass through probate are more likely to be contentious than estates that stay out of court. Appearing before a judge seems to bring out the worst in people.

Of course, the administrator of an estate that avoids probate still must follow the rules and carry out your written wishes—administrators can't just do whatever they want. I have had some clients question the advisability of planning to avoid probate, as they wonder whether their wishes are more likely to be followed by a judge. But managing an estate contrary to the written wishes of the deceased is illegal whether you're in court or not. That's stealing—just as bad as robbing a bank. Even estates that shouldn't have to go through probate might wind up in court if the administrator fails to follow the rules. This risk can be minimized if you make your written wishes excruciatingly clear. Leaving unclear or inconsistent instructions can be nearly as bad as leaving no instructions at all.

Princess Diana's will put her mother and sister in charge of her estate. Diana also left a letter that was quite specific about certain valuable personal property that she wanted her nieces, nephews, and godchildren to have. But the letter and the will were inconsistent, and the executors chose to ignore the letter, which led to a legal dispute. The court agreed with the executors' decision to ignore the letter, and Princess Diana's extended family received little from her estate.

Diana left written wishes, but she wasn't clear, and the family ended up fighting it out in court. You're doing your beneficiaries a huge favor if you are extremely specific. Having a written plan isn't enough. You need to be sure everyone knows what your plan means.

Once again, this is not a problem that ensnares only celebrities and others with large estates. Another case I handled involved a man who left behind two daughters and a longtime girlfriend. He left only a will, so his estate ended up in probate. The will named his daughters and girlfriend as equal beneficiaries, but it also contained a couple of specific distributions to other family members, one of which involved his "hand tools." We actually had to have a hearing because of a month-long disagreement about whether a gas-powered generator constituted a hand tool. The probate for this relatively small estate lasted well over a year, the bulk of the estate wound up going to creditors and attorney fees, and the family will never recover emotionally. A clearer plan, one that was written in a way that would have kept the estate out of probate court, could have prevented all of this.

In another case my firm handled, the deceased father had run a small service business for decades. He had a simple will that left everything to his two children. The estate and the plan were straightforward, but because everything had to go through probate court, the business he had spent his life building died with him. Each step of the probate process took so long that it was impossible for the family to keep the business in operation. No one had authority to hire employees to do the work, collect accounts receivable, or pay the bills. Even though there was money in the business account, the children couldn't access it without a court order, so the business was in default on several liabilities. If not for the drawn-out probate process, the children could have sold the business, but by the time they had the authority to act, the business was dead. They ended up selling off the equipment for pennies on the dollar to satisfy debts. This man thought his plan was sufficient: his estate wasn't large and his wishes were simple. But while everyone knew what he wanted, the legal requirements of the probate process prevented his plan from working the way he had envisioned, and his mistake proved quite costly to his children.

Neither of the cases my firm handled involved a large estate or complicated wishes, but the costs in terms of time and money were huge. In the first case, even worse was the permanent damage to family relationships caused by the probate process. Better planning could have avoided it. And all the fighting I've described played out in public. Probate is a court process, just like divorce and bankruptcy, and everything is public record. Every list of assets, every list of debts, every list of beneficiaries, and every disagreement wind up in the permanent court record. And the invasion of privacy extends beyond the court record. State law requires that you run a notice in the newspaper to announce the death of the person, tell the world that a probate has been opened, and invite any interested parties to formally make their claims. I have met with families who chose to abandon the property of a deceased family member because they knew creditors' claims would eat up the entire estate.

These real-life horror stories make the point that having to take an estate through probate means three big problems: lengthy delays, high costs, and a complete lack of privacy. In *all* probates.

Probate is a really slow process, usually lasting at least six months and often as long as a year even in straightforward cases. As you have seen, some of the bad ones can last several years. This waiting period is primarily for the benefit of creditors. The law does not want the probate closed and the estate distributed until everyone who claims a piece of the estate has been paid. You cannot simply file some papers and wrap the estate up tomorrow. You have to obtain the court's permission for almost everything you do.

Probate opens with an actual pleading, or a formal document, filed with the court. Based on the initial pleadings, the court appoints an executor to manage the estate. The executor then must go back to the judge for permission to handle every event that arises. If you are an executor and want to sell a house, for example, you have to present the court with the purchase contract and evidence of the fair market value of the house and ask the court for permission to execute the transaction. After the closing, you have to go back to the judge with a formal report of sale to verify that you did everything in accordance with the court's orders. This type of interaction continues throughout the probate until you get to the end, when you file a final petition asking for authority to pay all creditors who filed valid claims and to pay taxes, accountants, lawyers, and all other final expenses. Then you have to wait for the judge to determine how to divide whatever is left in the estate. Of course, if the deceased left a will, the judge will order that the remaining assets be distributed according to the instructions in the will. If there is no will, the relatives may fight about the interpretation of state statutes covering distribution of the estate. Even uncontested probates can be long and grueling simply because of the need to seek court permission at every turn.

Probate is also extremely expensive. The biggest expense usually is the attorney fees. Many states allow the lawyer who represents the estate to receive a percentage of the estate—in Arkansas, for example, 3 to 5 percent of the value of the property passing through probate may go to attorney fees under the statutory formula. (On an estate valued at $150,000, you would expect legal fees of about $5,000 under this formula.) Some lawyers choose not to accept the statutory fee, instead charging an hourly rate throughout the process, which can easily exceed the statutory percentage. Billing by the hour for anything but the simplest of probates can result in a fee of more than $10,000 even for modest estates.

Remember the man whose estate consisted of two forty-acre parcels and a house? How could his beneficiaries pay a legal fee with real estate? They couldn't. His family could not pay his bills until they sold his house. What happens in a probate involving a two-hundred-acre farm that has been in the family for generations? If that family has to put the farm through probate, and they don't want to sell it, how are they going to pay the probate fees? There's no good answer. And the legal fees are only part of the high costs of probate, which also entails court costs, publication fees, appraisal costs, accounting fees, and a host of other expenses. Cost is a real consideration.

Finally, probate is unpleasantly public. The lack of privacy comes from two general rules of probate. First, you must publish notice in a local paper announcing your business to the world. This is the notice that invites creditors to make claims against the estate and heirs to contest the will or otherwise claim their right to a share of the estate's assets. Second, everything submitted to the court throughout the entire process is open for anyone to inspect—and the probate process requires submitting many pleadings to the court.

Remember, these negative aspects of probate apply even in relatively simple, uncontested probates. It is well worth your time and money to put a plan in place to stay out of probate court.

Your estate will go somewhere when you die—it's not going with you. Like George Strait said, "I ain't never seen a hearse with a luggage rack." And if you don't plan, the path your estate will take to its destination will run through probate court. That's the rule, plain and simple.

I hope you take several lessons from the stories in this chapter about Elvis, Jimi Hendrix, and Princess Diana, as well as the real families I have worked with:

1. Having a will is better than not having a will, because counting on your family to know what you want isn't good enough. You must leave formal instructions in writing, and you'd better make those instructions crystal clear.
2. Having a will does not keep your estate out of probate court. A will is your set of instructions to the probate judge; it does nothing to keep you out of probate.
3. You don't want your family to have to take your estate through probate.

Maybe your primary motivation for planning is the emotional toll exacted by the probate process and the increased risk of disputes when a probate judge must oversee settlement of an estate. Or maybe the more tangible aspects—costs in terms of time and money or the complete lack of privacy—are what compel you to act. But by now, surely you see that taking steps to keep your estate out of probate court is the way to go.

Fortunately, you can use several techniques to keep your estate out of probate court. But you have to do it in advance. You must have a plan—one that fits your circumstances. The right plan for a young couple with small children will be different from the advice I'd give to a seventy-five-year-old worried about the costs of long-term care, to a sixty-five-year-old heading into retirement, or fifty-five-year-old newlyweds with grown children from previous marriages. No two plans are the same because every family's goals and priorities are different. But everyone needs a plan. There's still much to learn about planning for death—one of the only certainties in life—so turn to chapter 2 to learn the best ways to keep your estate out of probate court.

CHAPTER TWO

Avoiding Probate: The Primary Goal

Jimi Hendrix. Elvis. The stories of their probates made for lurid headlines. But I'll bet you didn't hear much at all about Ted Kennedy's estate.

Kennedy made what seem to have been wise decisions in his estate planning. He had the typical second marriage situation. When he died in 2009 at the age of seventy-seven, he wanted to leave part of his estate to his wife; they had been married for seventeen years. He wanted the rest of his estate to go to his children, who came from his first marriage. He included these wishes in a well-drafted trust.

If you put your second wife in charge of your trust, you risk alienating the children from your first marriage and creating conflict. But the likelihood of conflict may be just as high if you put one or more of the children in charge. My client from the first chapter, the one who left behind two daughters and a longtime girlfriend who fought over whether a gas-powered generator was a hand tool, ignored this potential problem. He put one of his daughters in charge of his estate, and you saw where they ended up. But Kennedy didn't name his wife as administrator, even though she was a top-notch attorney. Nor did he name his children. He named a family friend, Paul G. Kirk Jr., a former chair of the Democratic National Committee. He clearly was a trusted friend of Ted Kennedy's, because after Kennedy died, it was Kirk who held his senate seat until Massachusetts could hold a special election.

Kennedy's decision to use a trust to keep his estate out of probate and to draft it in a way that reduced the potential for conflict among his beneficiaries appears to have eliminated a lot of the troubles that can arise when a man's widow is his second wife. Had he not made wise planning decisions, you can bet you'd have heard about it.

Alas, not everyone is as smart as Ted Kennedy.

Using a trust is not the only way to keep an estate out of

probate, but it is often the best way, as Kennedy's story shows. Before they die, many people use deeds to transfer property to their children to keep that property out of probate. Certain types of deeds can be decent probate-avoiding tools if avoiding probate is your only goal, but using deeds comes with some risk. I once worked with a client who knew he needed a plan in order to keep his home out of probate, but he chose not to use a trust in his planning.

This client deeded his house to his three children. After his wife died, he figured, "I'll just get my property out of my name now because I know if anything's in my name when I die, it's going to wind up in probate." He was right about probate court and smart to plan to avoid it, but his decision to deed the property directly to his children backfired.

Several years after he signed that deed, he came to me with what he thought was a simple request: "I need you to change my deed. One of my children has died. I need to get his name off the deed to my home and put the property in the names of my other kids."

If only it were that simple. I had to tell him, "This property is not yours to redirect. We can't just give that one-third interest to your other children now. It belongs to your deceased son or, more accurately, to his estate."

As much as we strive to stay out of probate court, the only option at this point was to probate his son's estate. His probate was going to be a bit of a mess because he had a daughter, but his daughter—the granddaughter of my client—was well taken care of. She didn't really need a one-third interest in her grandfather's home. She was going to sign off on whatever we needed to do to accomplish her grandfather's plan, but it wasn't that easy. The bigger problem was her father's creditors. Her father had no insurance and huge medical bills at the end of his life, and the doctors and hospitals and other medical service providers would not let her simply sign her interest in the property over to her grandfather and close out her father's estate. They wanted to be paid. In the end, one of the surviving brothers had to literally buy this one-third interest from the estate of his deceased brother in order to protect their father's property.

So, yes, having property in your name at death can be a problem, because it's going to throw your estate into probate, but simply deeding property to your children can cause worse problems.

To be clear, you can, in fact, stay out of probate by deeding property while you're living; you just have to understand the pitfalls in this method of planning. And you should be aware that there's more than one type of deed in the world. The quitclaim deed is probably the most common. Basically, that's a deed that just says whatever interest I have in this property is now yours. Period.

A warranty deed is similar, in that it says whatever interest I have is yours, but it goes one step further: I commit to warrant and defend the title to the property when I sign a warranty deed. In essence, I promise that I have good title to the property, so you can be confident that you now have good title. A quitclaim deed does not carry that kind of promise.

Many states also have something called a life estate deed or something similar. With a life estate deed, I can transfer title to my property but still retain a life estate, which is the right to live on the property, use the property, earn income from the property, and benefit from the property in any way while I am living. Upon my death, my life estate terminates and full, unrestricted ownership vests with whomever I named in the deed—without going through probate, executing another deed, or requiring any additional legal work. Although it may seem like the person who holds the life estate holds all the power, there's one important thing a life estate holder can't do—sell or otherwise transfer an interest in the property to someone else. A life estate deed transfers ownership of the property to a new owner the moment it is signed. However, the new owner can't do much with the property she now owns because her interest is inferior to the interest of the life estate holder until that person dies. In order to sell property owned under a life estate deed, the life estate holder and the remainder owner named in the deed must work together.

The man who needed his surviving son to buy the one-third interest in his house from the estate of his deceased son actually had used a life estate deed in his planning. That's a good example of how life estate deeds carry with them risks similar to quitclaim and warranty deeds. The rights retained by life estate holders sometimes give them a false sense of security, making them feel as if they have not really transferred any interest in their property until they die. But that's just not the case.

Another type of deed often used to bypass probate court is called a beneficiary deed in Arkansas, but something similar exists in many states, although sometimes under another name. Unlike the other deeds I have discussed, a beneficiary deed does not transfer any interest in the property until the death of the owner who signed the deed, and the transfer is revocable right up until the time of death. Thus if I sign a beneficiary deed, all I'm saying is this property will be yours when I die, unless I change my mind and do something else with it. This type of deed would have been much safer for my client because, when his son died, he would still have had the authority to change his deed without having to reckon with the probate court overseeing his son's estate.

Another important thing to note about deeds is that multiple owners can jointly own property in a couple of different ways. The primary distinction is between joint ownership that carries survivorship rights and joint ownership that does not. In other words, if two people jointly hold title to property, and the deed says that they own that property with rights of survivorship, when one owner dies, the other becomes the sole remaining owner—no probate, new deed, or other legal work required. If the deed does not say that the joint ownership includes rights of survivorship, when one owner dies, the surviving owner still owns only a one-half interest in the property. The half interest held by the person who died goes to that person's estate and probably winds up in probate. This form of ownership is commonly referred to as tenancy in common. One form of ownership isn't always preferable to the other. In some cases, co-owners do not want to include survivorship rights in a deed. They want to ensure that their interest in the property passes to their family instead of the other co-owners. The key to remember, then, is that when a deed does not include survivorship rights between co-owners, the co-owners must take other steps to keep their interests in the property out of probate.

Survivorship rights are almost always desirable when a married couple owns property jointly. In fact, in Arkansas, the law assumes that a deed to property owned by a married people carries with it survivorship rights, even if the deed does not include language to that effect. This rule often keeps surviving spouses out of probate court, even if the couple failed to engage in any planning. So long as the surviving spouse's name appears on the deed, no probate is required, at least for the house. This rule also gives many surviving spouses a false sense of security, however. Some people think, "I didn't have to go through probate when my spouse died; I assume that will be the case when I die." But that's a false assumption.

Similar rules apply to bank accounts. You can have more than one name on a bank account, whether it's the names of both spouses, mother and son, or father and daughter. Jointly owned bank accounts do not go through probate so long as one of the co-owners is alive. The danger of intentionally opening a joint account outside a marriage—say, when a mother adds her daughter to her account—is that you open that account up to the legal risks of all the people whose names you may choose to put on your account (if the daughter lives beyond her means, Mom is likely to have to pay her daughter's creditors). This is the same type of risk that caught my client whose dead son's name was on his deed. His surviving son didn't have to save his father's property from his father's creditors but from his dead brother's.

People run into this type of problem all the time with bank accounts. They think, "For convenience, I'm going to add my son or daughter to my checking account so that if anything happens to me, they can write checks and pay my bills." The problem is that now that account is vulnerable to any and all risks that child may have—a bankruptcy or a divorce or a lawsuit. Note that none of those situations assumes your child deliberately harmed you in any way. I'm not talking about the risks associated with intentional wrongdoing by a child, such as helping himself to money from your account without your permission—which he could well do if he was a joint owner. I'm talking about things that your child has no control over, third parties that come after your child for debts she may not even owe. Anything that has that child's name on it is fair game.

A similar but much safer technique for bank accounts is something commonly referred to as a POD (payable on death) designation. This is basically an agreement between the bank and you as an account holder that says, "While I'm alive, this is my account. When I die, I want this account to pass directly to the listed individuals."

This type of planning can work with any type of bank account—checking, savings, money markets, and certificates of deposit.

Using a POD designation does not mean your accounts belong to your heirs while you are living, so this type of planning does not open you up to all their legal risks. The funds do not become theirs until you die. To gain access to the account, all they have to do is go to the bank, formally identify themselves, and present a copy of your death certificate. A POD designation can be a reasonably safe way to avoid probate with modest assets.

Other types of financial accounts, such as brokerage accounts, retirement accounts, annuities, and stocks, can pass to your heirs through beneficiary designations, too, but financial institutions do not refer to those designations as POD designations. They may be called TOD (transfer on death) designations or simply death beneficiary designations.

Life insurance policies rarely go through probate. With a life insurance policy, you have a contract with a life insurance company that says when I'm gone, here's where I want the money from this policy to go—it's pretty straightforward in most cases. One problem I've seen is that people fail to keep the beneficiary designations up to date. Say one spouse names the other as the death beneficiary on his life insurance, but then the beneficiary of the policy dies first. The surviving spouse doesn't remember that he needs to take some steps to clean up his estate. When he dies, the only beneficiary on his policy is his late spouse, so the policy winds up in probate. That's why I say life insurance typically doesn't go through probate, but if you're not diligent in keeping things up to date, a life insurance policy could wind up there. The same type of problem can present itself when using POD, TOD, and other death beneficiary designations. You must be diligent in keeping designations up to date.

Let me recap briefly: A last will and testament, probably the most common estate-planning tool, will not allow your estate to bypass probate. A last will and testament is your set of instructions to the probate court, telling the judge, "Here's what I want to happen when I'm dead." Having a will is better than not having a will, because if you don't leave any instructions, the probate judge doesn't know your wishes; not having a will invites fighting and disagreement by your nearest and dearest and forces the judge to rely on state statutes to decide who gets what.

To avoid probate, some planners will use one of the types of deeds I mentioned earlier along with co-ownership arrangements or death beneficiary designations on financial accounts and life insurance. But, as you've seen, that type of planning can be risky. It's also inflexible and leaves you unable to protect your heirs from themselves (when necessary because of age or inability to manage money) and from others who might try to get their hands on your children's inheritance (such as creditors, divorcing spouses, and litigation opponents). I'll get into this issue in more detail in chapter 3, but first you need to learn the basics of another estate-planning option—trusts.

Some people become nervous or scared when they hear me talk about trusts. They think they have to have millions before they should consider using a trust, but in a lot of respects, a trust is just a will replacement that keeps your estate out of probate and offers you a lot of flexibility in your planning.

A trust, like a will, is a set of instructions for what should happen when you die. The biggest difference is that those instructions are not for a judge in probate court. If you have a trust, carrying out your instructions will not require lawyers, courts, or judges. It's nothing scary, and it doesn't have to be confusing or complicated.

Both trusts and wills have three main players. The first is the person who creates the instrument, which for a will that person is often called the testator, and the person who creates a trust is called the grantor (because this is who grants property to the trust). The grantor of a trust usually retains certain powers in connection with the trust and the trust property. In many trusts, the grantor retains the right to add property to the trust, remove property from the trust, amend and modify the trust, or do away with the trust altogether.

The second player in a will is the executor, the person with the task of executing your wishes in probate court. Trusts have a similar role, that of trustee. Your trustee is the person who has the authority to manage the trust. Just as the president of a business runs the business, the trustee of a trust runs the trust. Trustees are restricted. They can do only what the terms of the trust allow them to do. The grantor who created the trust and the trustee who manages the trust can be, and often is, the same person. But all trusts will appoint a successor trustee to take over management of the trust when the original trustee dies or becomes incapacitated. If the grantor and the trustee are not the same person, the grantor has more power than the trustee, because the grantor sets all the rules for the trustee and, depending on the type of trust involved, can usually remove the trustee for any reason.

The third player in a will and in a trust is the beneficiary, or the person who will benefit from the property. Grantors can give one set of beneficiaries the right to use and benefit from the trust property while the grantors are living and a different set of beneficiaries the right to receive the property upon the death of the grantors. The beneficiaries during the lifetimes of the grantors are often the grantors themselves. The grantors might set up a trust for their own benefit while they are living, but they'll always name a death beneficiary to receive or otherwise benefit from the property after the grantors have died.

Let me say that again. In many trusts, the grantor, the initial trustee, and the lifetime beneficiary are all the same person. I especially stress this point to clients who fear that setting up a trust means giving up authority to manage or use the trust property.

After the death of the lifetime beneficiary, who is often the grantor of the trust, the successor trustee could be one of the beneficiaries but may not be. If the grantors want some checks and balances so that the people benefiting from the trust are not the same people managing the trust, the grantors could name trustees who are not also beneficiaries. The owner of a more substantial estate—one that holds enough value to warrant payment of management fees—might name a professional trustee, often referred to as a corporate fiduciary, to manage the trust. A corporate fiduciary is often a business, such as the trust department of a bank or a division of a financial institution, that is licensed and bonded to manage trusts, and its employees are specially trained in trust management. These companies, of course, do charge a fee for this service, but the fee is often earned many times over by the skill they bring to managing and administering the trust assets.

In middle-class America, it is much more common to name an individual as trustee whenever possible, perhaps one or more of the grantor's children or a sibling or a trusted family friend, someone who typically doesn't charge a fee to manage the trust. These trustees carry out your wishes as a last expression of their friendship or of their relationship with you or because they also are one of the beneficiaries named in the trust.

Sometimes one child is more suited to serve as trustee than the others. Say a couple has three children, one of whom is an accountant and great with money. She's got the complete trust of the parents, whereas the other children have been through bankruptcy, have been married several times, or have trouble paying their bills. In that case the parents will name the accountant daughter as the trustee, but all three kids can still benefit from the trust. It's just that two of them will not have any control of the trust.

Because wills and trusts are so similar, a lot of people don't see why a trust avoids probate while a will does not—what's the difference? Well, when you set up a trust, you have to take one additional step that you don't take with a will. This is the step my grandparents did not know about (see the introduction), and they are not alone. I call it trust funding.

To recap: My grandparents hired a lawyer to draw up a trust for them. They signed it and had it notarized, and the lawyer put it in a binder and sent them home with it. But my grandparents missed an essential step in trust planning: they never changed the title to their property so that the trust owned that property.

Having a trust will do nothing for you if you don't fund that trust. You have to change the deed to your house so that instead of saying, "Jane and John Smith, a married couple," it says, "Jane and John Smith, as trustees of the Smith Living Trust." It's not a big change on paper but actually a really big change in the legal effect of that deed. You would also tell each bank and brokerage firm you use that you have a trust and have them either retitle your accounts into the name of the trust or set the accounts to pay to your trust upon your death. Otherwise, those accounts are not part of that trust, may not pass according to your wishes, and will probably wind up in probate.

That's the part my grandparents didn't do. They didn't fund their trust—they didn't retitle their home and rental property so that they became part of the trust—and as a result, the trust was no help at all in avoiding probate. And they have some famous companions in that trap.

After Michael Jackson died in June 2009, lawyers for his mother filed probate papers saying that he had died without a will or a trust, and she gained temporary control of his estate; she also had temporary custody of his three children.

Shortly thereafter, a lawyer produced a 2002 will signed by Jackson that also established the Michael Jackson Family Trust. The will named the lawyer, Jackson's accountant, and a longtime record industry associate of Jackson's as coexecutors of his will and trustees of the family trust. Jackson's mother was not named to either role, so she lost control of the estate. The interesting thing, though, is that none of the entertainer's assets were ever moved into the trust before he died.

The main people who benefited from that arrangement were the lawyers who took his estate through probate. By September 2012, when Jackson's assets still had not been moved into the trust, his estate had generated more than $600 million since his death, the Associated Press reported in June 2014. In fact, according to a story earlier that year in the *Los Angeles Times*, the IRS claimed in U.S. Tax Court filings that, at the time of his death, Jackson was worth $1.125 billion, not the $7 million his executors claimed in initial probate pleadings. As this book went to press, it appeared that his trust had not yet been funded and that the estate would be in court for many years to come, all the while generating fees for lawyers and non-family executors and trustees.

The moral to this story? Having a great trust and expensive lawyers doesn't keep you out of probate if you don't take that next step and fund the trust. Remember the point of chapter 1? If you have assets *in your name* when you die, you wind up in probate court. When you use a trust, you get your assets out of your name without giving those assets to your heirs too soon. That's what funding is all about, and it's the reason a trust keeps your estate out of probate while a will does not.

Now that you have a better idea of what a trust is and how it works, you should realize one more thing about trusts: two very different types of trust are available to you—revocable and irrevocable—and which one you choose depends on your priorities.

A revocable trust can be changed or modified at any time

so long as the grantor has the capacity to do so. That is, so long as you have the ability to understand what you're doing and why you're doing it, you can change a revocable trust, making it one of the most flexible estate-planning tools available to you. An irrevocable trust is more set in stone. Once you establish the terms for an irrevocable trust, changing or modifying the terms is difficult. This does not mean that the assets held by an irrevocable trust can't change or that the trustee can't gain access to them if necessary, but the trust document itself cannot be amended or terminated.

So if a revocable trust is extremely flexible and an irrevocable trust is not, why would anyone want an irrevocable trust? Typically, that type of trust is much more beneficial if your top priority is protecting assets from long-term care expenses. This is one of the places where the first strand of planning—getting your assets where you want them to go without probate—intertwines with the third strand of planning—making sure there's something left for your beneficiaries to inherit when you're gone.

As I said earlier, it's all about your priorities. If your top priority is flexibility in your planning, then you want a revocable trust. If your top priority is sheltering assets from long-term care expenses, an irrevocable trust is perhaps the better way to go. Both have pros and cons, and I'll explore them in part 3.

I want to return to something I mentioned briefly in the discussion of revocable and irrevocable trusts. I said that a revocable trust can be changed or modified at any time *so long as the grantor has the capacity to do so.* Using a trust is a good way to plan for incapacity—the time when you're no longer able to manage your own affairs because of age or illness. You have already learned that all trusts should name a successor trustee, someone who can take over trust management when the initial trustee can no longer serve in that role. Most people think about the successor trustee only in connection with the death of the initial trustee, but the successor can also be a lifesaver in the event of incapacity. However, the successor trustee can take over only trust-related business. Another set of documents is necessary to manage affairs that are unrelated to the trust—power-of-attorney documents.

Families can execute a perfect plan to stay out of probate court at death but unintentionally wind up in court anyway if they don't plan for the possibility of incapacity. The risk here is guardianship court.

Guardianship has nothing to do with dying people. Guardianship is a legal procedure that some families are forced to use when a family member is no longer able to make or communicate rational decisions. Because of a mental or physical disability or just plain old age, the person no longer has the ability to manage his own affairs. His family winds up in guardianship court because the now-disabled person never nominated another person to step in and take care of his affairs in those situations.

Granting a power of attorney to someone to step in and take care of your affairs if you're not able to manage them yourself is just as important as setting up a trust to stay out of probate court. To keep you and your family out of guardianship court in the event you are incapacitated, you will want to give someone a general durable power of attorney to deal with business and financial affairs and a health-care power of attorney to deal with your medical professionals.

Some people are hesitant to sign a power of attorney because they think, "Once I sign the power of attorney, I'm basically saying I can't manage my own affairs anymore." No. That is not what power of attorney says. Some people think, "I'm signing away my life. I no longer have authority to do a thing." That's also not what a power of attorney does.

The power of attorney simply nominates someone to do things for you if and when you're not able to do things for yourself. A power of attorney cannot override your wishes. In most instances, a power of attorney is completely revocable, so if you name someone to hold power of attorney and decide you'd rather give someone else that power, you always have the ability to change it.

When someone goes through life without ever nominating someone to serve as power of attorney or as health-care power of attorney, that person is playing a high-risk game, because they're just one health event, one car wreck, one accident away from being in a position where they can't make decisions for themselves but no one else can, either.

Naming someone as your power of attorney is the best way to deal with bank accounts, not by adding a child to a bank account as a co-owner so they can pay your bills for you. Your power of attorney can legally sign checks for you as your representative without being co-owner of the account and without all the risks associated with co-ownership arrangements.

On the medical side I always remind clients about the sad case of Terri Schiavo in Florida. She was twenty-six in 1990 when she suffered heart failure that led to severe brain damage, a health event that no one could see coming. She ended up in a coma. Her husband and parents fought a seven-year court battle that was very political and very public, because they disagreed about whether, as her husband said, she did not want to be kept alive by artificial means, or whether, as her parents said, she wanted to be given a chance to recover (she had already been in a coma for eight years when the legal battle began). But I'm not bringing this up to foment yet another debate about end-of-life care and the right to die.

The point is simply this: If she had given someone her health-care power of attorney, which would have given that person legal authority to make important decisions for her, there would not have been a seven-year court battle that went to the U.S. Supreme Court or an intervention by the governor of Florida. I can't say everyone would have been happy with the decisions made. If she had named her husband as power of attorney, it is reasonable to assume that her grieving parents would still have sought to challenge his decisions. But at least, the person making the decisions would have been the person she chose when she had the ability to do so, and he would have had the legal support of her power-of-attorney documents when he was trying to manage her affairs. An even more definitive instruction is the advance directive, a document stating the signer's wishes regarding end-of-life care.

In the first chapter, you saw how important it is to plan ahead to stay out of probate, and now you have learned that there is more than one way to do that. If you choose to use deeds and death beneficiary designations to avoid probate, do so with knowledge of the risks and limitations related to that type of planning. And remember, you must address each and every asset if you want to stay out of probate court. Putting a death beneficiary designation on each of your financial accounts won't keep you out of probate court if your house is still in your name when you die.

If you choose to use a trust to avoid probate, let my grandparents' story remind you that the best trust in the world won't keep you out of probate if you don't properly fund it. Unfortunately, as Michael Jackson's story shows, you can't rely on your estate-planning attorney to remind you of the importance of funding. And by all means, whether you're young or old, rich or poor, married or single, take the time to sign power-of-attorney documents. Avoiding probate is important, but the truth is, by the time probate becomes an issue, you'll be dead. Failing to plan for incapacity can have a big impact on your finances and your quality of life.

In chapter 3, I'll dig a little deeper into using trusts in estate planning to do more than stay out of probate court, the first strand of good planning, and I'll tell you about some planning opportunities you probably have never even considered. If you're going to take the time and spend the money to get your affairs in order, you might as well do it right. Failure to consider the lessons of chapter 3 could turn your gift into a curse.

CHAPTER THREE

Devil in the Details: The Gremlin Problem

———

Remember *Gremlins*, the 1984 Christmas movie that was both a comedy and a horror flick? In the film, Rand, a struggling inventor, wants to give his son, Billy, a memorable Christmas present. At a Chinatown antique store, he finds a small, furry creature called a mogwai. The owner of the store refuses to sell it to Rand, but the owner's young grandson is less cautious. He secretly sells the mogwai to Rand, telling him to pay attention to three important rules: do not expose the mogwai to sunlight; do not let it get wet, and never feed it after midnight. Rand proudly gives the creature to Billy, who treats it as a pet and names it Gizmo.

Predictably, Billy is too young to abide by the rules. He quickly learns that when mogwai get wet, they spawn more mogwai. At first, having more mogwai doesn't seem like a problem. Sure, there are a lot of them, but they are sweet little fur balls. Billy thinks he can manage. But feeding a mogwai after midnight is a much bigger deal. After the mogwai trick Billy into letting them eat after midnight, they turn into cocoons from which they later emerge as mischievous, reptilian gremlins that enjoy causing trouble and will even torture and kill for fun.

In the end, Billy and Gizmo succeed in killing what had become an army of gremlins but not before the gremlins destroyed the entire town and killed several innocent people. Near the end of the movie, the owner of the Chinatown antique store shows up to collect Gizmo. The storeowner observes that although Billy obviously is not currently ready to care for something like Gizmo, one day Billy might be mature enough to handle that kind of responsibility (leaving open the possibility of a sequel).

Although you probably wouldn't think of *Gremlins* as a movie filled with important life lessons, it delivers one message that we would be wise to keep in mind when planning our estates: it is essential that you consider whether your heirs are ready, willing, and able to manage their inheritance properly. A gift can quickly turn into a curse when given to someone who, like Billy in the movie, is not equipped to handle it.

The reality is that there is more to estate planning than simply deciding to set up a trust and settling on which type of trust best fits your situation. Establishing a trust means you will need to make several other decisions. First, you have to fill the two key roles in a trust—trustee and beneficiary. In other words, you have to decide who will manage the trust and who will inherit your property. Second, you have to think about how you want to convey your estate to your beneficiaries so that what you intend as a gift does not become a curse.

This is especially important for parents of young children. When I meet these parents, they sometimes tell me, "We don't have a lot yet. We're just starting out in life. We recently bought a home, but we have a big mortgage. And we have only a little bit of money in the bank." They've given no thought to setting up a trust. If they do think about the future at all, they take out some life insurance, and they might consider having wills drawn up just to name a guardian for their children in case both parents die. These young parents are being smart—life insurance is probably a good idea when you have young children, and they really do need to name a guardian for them. Otherwise, the kids could end up in the middle of a custody battle fought by different sides of the family, each believing that they'd be the relatives better able to raise your children.

So if you are parents of young children, you absolutely need to sign documents naming a guardian who is to have physical custody of your children. But you also need to set up a trust because you can't pass your estate directly to minors. Children younger than eighteen cannot legally own property. And even if you as young parents don't have a lot of assets now, you could have considerably more when you die—maybe life insurance proceeds, equity in the house, or even proceeds from a settlement if someone was legally at fault in your death.

Some people think they have a simple solution to this problem. They will tell me, "I'll leave everything to my mom because I know she'll do what's right and take care of my kids." I hope she would; she's your mother. But that's not the way to do it. Counting on her to somehow figure out what you would have wanted her to do just isn't fair. Not to mention all the legal and tax problems you might cause by using that type of plan. In any case, you have to do some planning to make sure your estate doesn't wind up in probate court before it gets to your mother, so why not do it the right way?

The better approach is to create a trust that names your

children as the beneficiaries. If they are minors, they are not put in charge of the trust and they do not receive the property outright when you die. The property stays in trust for their benefit, and a person of your choosing—someone you can rely on or a corporate fiduciary—would manage those trust assets according to your wishes. For example, the trust my wife and I established says that if we die and our children are not yet thirty years old, we want everything to remain in trust to be managed by our parents. Of course, no matter what age our children might be when we die, our trustees could use the funds for our children's health care and education. And they could use the funds to make sure our kids are well taken care of. But our trust specifies that our trustees cannot give our children the money directly. The trustees are to treat our children the way that we would have treated them—do for them what we would have done until they are older and can manage their inheritance themselves.

When each child reaches the age of twenty-five or graduates from college, whichever occurs first, that child will receive half of his or her inheritance outright. They can do with it as they see fit. Then, just in case they make a mistake and blow it all, we give them a second chance when they turn thirty, when they can receive the other half of their inheritance outright. You can do all sorts of creative things like this with your trust, such as encouraging your kids to go to college by saying they can't get a penny from the trust until they graduate. There are several ways to encourage them in a certain direction, even in your absence, through the terms of your trust.

I think that even eighteen is too young for someone to receive a large sum of money. I think that until children are older, say, twenty-five or thirty, they need some protection. You can guide their decisions by using the trust as encouragement while also making sure they are protected. With minor children, especially young children, you almost have to use a trust to leave them anything at all.

Sometimes children have health issues that demand even more detailed planning. Parents with children who are disabled now or likely to be on some form of disability payments in the future need to be even more cautious to ensure these children are able to continue receiving any disability and health benefits to which they might be entitled now and in the future. Many benefit programs designed to help those with disabilities, such as Supplemental Security Income and Medicaid, have strict income and asset limits. Receiving an inheritance in the wrong way will disqualify a disabled person for those programs. If you are the parent of a disabled child, you can establish a special needs trust for that child (sometimes called a supplemental needs trust); it will protect the child's eligibility for government benefits while also protecting the child from the pitfalls more typical trusts address, such as creditors and poor money management.

With a special needs trust, the child is the beneficiary named in the document, and the trust assets can be used only for that beneficiary, but the assets don't really belong to the beneficiary, nor are they controlled by the beneficiary. A trustee, who cannot be the beneficiary, is appointed as manager of the funds. The trustee cannot give money directly to the beneficiary but can use the funds with few restrictions to meet the needs (and in most cases the desires) of the beneficiary.

But what about planners who do not have young children or disabled beneficiaries to protect? What if you have adult children—thirty or forty or even fifty years old—and, if you are honest with yourself, you know that they are not really capable of managing a significant amount of money? We've all read plenty of stories about people who win the lottery and a year later are worse off than they were before. People who are not financially stable or responsible can wind up in big trouble after they receive an inheritance, even if they don't make horrible decisions themselves. This ties into what I was saying in chapter 2 about the inadvisability of adding children's names to your bank accounts.

Say your child has done nothing wrong, but after receiving her inheritance from your estate, she ends up in divorce court or in trouble with creditors or someone sues her after breaking a leg on her property. The money your daughter inherited from you could become fair game. If it flowed from your estate into her personal accounts, it becomes her personal asset, and it could be sucked right into any sort of legal problem that your daughter may have.

If, on the other hand, the inheritance remains in trust for your children's benefit, even if they are thirty or forty or fifty, the assets can be sheltered from your children's legal problems. If you're comfortable with it, you can still allow your children to serve as their own trustees to manage their shares of the inheritance, and those assets will remain sheltered from outside threats. If you're not comfortable with that—if you fear they'd have no idea how to manage an inheritance and would blow it in a second, even without attacks from creditors or divorcing spouses— you can put someone else in charge of your children's inheritance, no matter their age. In other words, you can protect them from themselves; you can protect them from others, or you can protect them from both themselves and others, depending on how you set up your trust.

Some trusts specify, "My trustee is to ensure that my heirs are contributing members of society and may receive the money only if they are working and fully employed." Such a clause can be especially useful if you have concerns that a beneficiary will think, "Now that I've inherited this money, I can stop working and live off my inheritance." You'd be surprised—I'm not talking about people whose parents were multimillionaires. Some people will inherit $100,000 and decide they're going to stop working, live off the money till it's gone, and then go back to work.

Unlike Rand, if you plan wisely, you are not giving your child a gremlin—that is, an asset that you know your child may not be able to take care of. Perhaps your child is not mature enough or sophisticated enough to take care of it. You are still ensuring your estate winds up where you want it to go, but you are getting it there safely, sheltered, and properly management.

Thus deciding to establish a trust is only the first decision you need to make. After making that important decision, you must ask yourself several follow-up questions: Do I need to be creative about the terms? Do I have minor children I need to protect? Do I have disabled children I need to look out for? Do I have adult children who need protection from themselves or from others who would go after their inheritance? The boilerplate language in typical trust forms is not sufficient to address such concerns. And the basic payable-on-death designations, co-ownership arrangements, and deed options I discussed in chapter 2 do not offer the type of protection you are looking for. With a properly drafted trust, you have control over how, when, and under what circumstances your estate passes to your beneficiaries, how it's used, and who can get their hands on it.

The story of Marilyn Monroe's estate provides another good example of the utility of trusts. Her estate wound up in the hands of a total stranger. What happened after she died was not anything she could have predicted. However, she could have avoided an undesirable outcome by planning just a little bit better.

She died in 1962, and she did leave a will, but she didn't have a trust. Her will asked the probate court to create a trust to care for her ailing mother, who had spent most of her adult life in a mental institution. Again, Monroe could have done this outside probate court by creating a trust while she was living.

The biggest portion of Marilyn Monroe's estate went to her acting coach, Lee Strasberg, who at the time was married to Paula, his second wife and also an acting coach. They were like surrogate parents to Monroe, and their daughter, Susan, was a close friend of Marilyn's. Monroe loved the Strasbergs and wanted her estate to benefit them, so after setting aside a small share for her mother, she left everything directly to Lee in her will. But when Lee Strasberg died in 1982, his entire estate went to his surviving spouse, who—you guessed it—was not Paula, who had died in 1966. When he died, Lee was married to Anna, a Venezuela-born actor.

Marilyn Monroe never knew Anna, but because Monroe left almost everything directly to Lee Strasberg, and he left everything to Anna, most of Monroe's estate wound up in Anna Strasberg's hands. She sold everything off, all the personal things, all the sentimental things. She also hired a firm that manages the estates of dead celebrities and made a ton of money from the rights to Marilyn Monroe's brand and image. Anna Strasberg subsequently sold the firm created to manage those rights for an estimated $20 million to $30 million. She got this windfall only because she was married to Lee Strasberg when he died.

This is a good example of why it is important to think about how you leave your estate to those you care about. Suppose I leave my entire estate to my son, who is married to someone I like quite well, but shortly after my death, he divorces and marries someone else. Although I would have wanted my grandkids to inherit everything of mine when my son dies, he executes an estate plan that directs all his assets to his new wife. So my entire bequest is redirected because I didn't put any restrictions on my son. I just left everything to him.

In a well-drafted trust, you can and should specify what happens to your assets when your beneficiaries die. Your instructions can protect your estate while it's in the hands of your beneficiaries and direct what happens to your estate if your beneficiaries die before or after you. Many of my clients specify that their assets are not to pass to a son- or daughter-in-law if their daughter or son is not alive to benefit from my client's estate.

Despite all these caveats, some people insist, "I just want the simplest plan possible. I'll just put everything in my kids' names." My position is, if you are aware of all the negative consequences that could result from a plan like that and you still want to do it that way, that's fine. You're the client, and you should do what you think is best, but it's my job—and the job of any good estate-planning attorney—to make sure you think about all the ramifications and help you find the best option, given your specific goals and priorities.

Beyond worrying about how and when money goes to your beneficiaries, there's one more important consideration. One of your goals should be to avoid doing anything that will cause family fights when you're gone. When preparing trusts and other estate-planning documents, people sometimes make decisions that are almost certain to lead to disagreements and animosity.

To draw on an example I used earlier, say you have three children, and you consider one to be a lot more prudent with money than the others. You make that child the trustee for all three shares. But what you've done is put one child in a position of authority over the others and set the stage for one of two things to happen. The child who is in charge may simply ignore your wishes and give the imprudent children anything they ask for because, as she tells them, "I don't want to fight with you. Here—just take your part," which was not what you wanted. Or the trustee may try to follow your wishes and—surprise, surprise—the children end up hating each other. Sometimes, when you have more than one child, naming just one as the administrator is a bad idea.

However, I've seen bad stories on the other side of that decision, too, where my client either couldn't decide which child to name to an important management role or didn't want to appear to favor one over the others. One interesting example involves an older client of mine who was setting up power-of-attorney documents. She had five children and insisted on naming all five as coagents on her health-care power of attorney, each with independent authority to act on her behalf.

I told her, "That's not a good idea. Think about the too-many-cooks-in-the-kitchen thing. We're going to mess up the recipe. If everybody's in charge, nobody will be in charge—they may not agree on what to do, and they're all going to fight in the end."

She said, "Nope, I can't decide. I want all five on there." Several years passed, and it was not an issue. But then she had to enter a skilled nursing facility because of her age and illnesses. Two of her five children were involved as primary caregivers. They had found the facility for her, and they had the most interactions with the nurses and the doctors there.

One primary caregiver called me in a panic one day and said, "Our other three siblings are tired of this nursing home. We don't know what happened. We still think it's the best place for Mom; she's comfortable there. But they are actually on their way up there right now to pick her up. We got a call from the nursing home. What can we do?"

I had to tell them, "You really can't do much because their power of attorney is just as strong as yours is." The daughter replied, "I don't understand. What do we do?"

"Tell the nursing home to keep her room ready," I said. "Keep her bed warm."

"Why?"

"Because once she's at her new facility, you have just as much authority to show up at the new facility, pick her up, and take her back."

The woman who called me said, "This is horrible. We don't want her bounced back and forth between facilities."

"I know," I said. "That's why we prefer fewer agents listed on a power of attorney in situations like this. Your mother couldn't make up her mind, so I'm going to have to give you the name and number of a good guardianship attorney, and y'all are going to have to go fight it out in court. It'll be up to a judge if you guys can't agree what to do."

That's what happens if you try to name too many people as power of attorney. You wind up in guardianship court anyway because they can't get along. The same thing happens with a trust that has too many trustees. But if you put one child in charge of the finances of another, chances are good that they won't be able to get along. So what's the solution? To tell you the truth, there's no perfect answer that works in all cases. It depends on your family. Sometimes you simply have to make what might be a tough decision and name one child as trustee even though that decision could hurt another child's feelings.

In your case, maybe a joint trustee arrangement could work out. And sometimes you simply have to be practical and put someone from outside the immediate family in charge, as Ted Kennedy decided to do.

In some cases, the only good option is to name a corporate fiduciary, such as the trust department at your bank or another financial institution, to manage the finances for your trust after you are gone. They charge a small percentage of the assets they manage, but you need to understand that they are probably going to manage the assets more intelligently—and certainly more dispassionately—than your heirs would. A corporate fiduciary will probably save money in the long run, even though it is charging a management fee. And even if it doesn't, if using a corporate fiduciary saves relationships between your family members, it was worth it.

The point of this chapter is not to make your estate planning more complicated than it needs to be, but I would be doing you a disservice if I didn't point out the devil in the details; the places where planning can go awry. Many discussions on estate planning end where chapter 2 left off—you really want to avoid probate court, and here are some ways to do that—out of fear that going further will scare people into postponing their planning. Certainly, the key first step is deciding to plan ahead to avoid probate and having the know-how to do it properly. But an essential second step is putting enough thought into your plan so that it does more than keep your estate out of probate. You want a *good* plan—a plan that protects your beneficiaries from themselves and others, preserves disabled heirs' eligibility for government benefits, ensures the assets are managed competently, and preserves family harmony. That's what this chapter is all about.

People are always at their worst when they lose a family member, especially when money is involved. Don't be naive. If leaving money directly to your children is a bad idea, don't do it. If you know one of your heirs shouldn't be managing your estate, don't put him in charge. You can benefit your heirs without turning your gift into a curse. All it takes is some planning.

No matter your age, and no matter your circumstances, it feels good to have a plan and to have your affairs in order. It feels even better to have a *good* plan, one that really takes into account your priorities and your specific circumstances. One of the only certainties in life is death, and the first strand of planning is all about ensuring that the assets you worked so hard to accumulate go where you want them to go in the way you want them to get there when you're gone.

But remember: Death is not the only certainty in life. The second strand of planning focuses on taxes. Don't forget my warning—you cannot look at one strand of planning and ignore the others. When you do that, you're likely to solve one problem but cause several others. A wise planner will recognize how the three strands of planning intertwine, and a strong plan will take all three strands into consideration.

Having read part 1, you understand why you should plan to avoid probate; you also have the know-how to do it and awareness of the additional details that go into a solid estate plan. But you also need to understand the tax implications of the decisions you will make. In part 2, I'll put your mind at ease regarding estate and gift taxes. The simple truth is that for most people, estate and gift taxes are red herrings that distract them from areas of planning that deserve much more attention. While most readers need not worry about estate and gift taxes, nearly everyone has to watch out for other tax traps, such as capital gains. The good news is that an educated planner can avoid them with ease, as I explain in part 2.

PART II

The Second Strand: Tax Considerations

(Or How to Give Less to the Government)

CHAPTER FOUR

Estate and Gift Taxes: A Red Herring

New clients frequently tell me, "I want to transfer some money to my grandchildren for college, but I have heard that I can't give them more than $14,000 each this year, because if I do, they are going to have to pay taxes on it." A lot of people think that—in fact, many tell me they heard about that $14,000 limit from their accountant, but they heard only part of what their accountant was trying to tell them. Or people tell me, "I need to get a will drawn up so that my family won't have to pay estate taxes."

The first client knows just enough to be dangerous. The

second one is really confused, for some reason thinking that a will is somehow going to spare beneficiaries from having to pay estate taxes. Estate-planning attorneys regularly see people who are extremely confused about what the estate tax is, what the gift tax is, and who has to pay them. The result is that people feel their top priority should be making sure they give some money to their kids or grandkids but not too much. Or that they need to take extreme measures to avoid paying an inheritance tax. And this often comes from people who do not have huge estates—maybe just a house and some modest financial accounts. Typically, my advice is not what they were expecting when they walked in the door. "Don't worry about that," I tell them. "You're looking at the wrong thing. You're worried about something that's totally irrelevant in your situation."

The estate tax and the gift tax are actually two different taxes, but they are tied together by IRS rules. I'm not an accountant, and I'm not going to be filing tax returns for anybody. But I can tell almost every client who walks through my door that the estate and gift taxes should be the last things they worry about when planning their estates. Everybody in the country has an exclusion amount—tied to both estates and lifetime gifts—that is now nearly $5.5 million for an individual and nearly $11 million for a couple, and the exclusion increases every year with inflation. That means that you can either give away that much in your lifetime without worrying about the gift tax or pass on an inheritance of that size before you even need to think about the estate tax.

When I say that the gift tax and the estate tax exemptions are tied together, what I mean is that when you use up your gift tax exemption by making reportable gifts during your lifetime, you not only reduce your lifetime gift tax exemption, you reduce your final estate tax exemption at the same time. In fact, many people refer to the $5.5 million exemption as a "combined exemption" because you receive only one exemption amount, but it is applicable to both lifetime gifts and estates. But if your combined reportable lifetime gifts and your final estate remain below the exemption amount at the time of your death, you will pay no gift or estate taxes. The vast majority of people I meet fall into this category. In fact, after hearing my explanation of the estate and gift taxes, most of my clients laugh. They can't believe they were worried about those taxes.

I used the term *reportable gift* in that explanation. That term addresses one of the more pointed questions that I hear. "What about the $14,000 limit? You say I can give away almost $5.5 million before worrying about the gift tax, but I am certain my accountant told me I need to keep my gifts under $14,000 per person per year." The best way to describe that $14,000 rule is that it is simply a *reporting* limit. In other words, if you give more than $14,000 in value—whether a house, land, money, stocks— to one person in one year while you are alive, you, *not the recipient*, are supposed to file a gift tax return to report the gift to the IRS. The IRS believes it is important that it keep track of gifts of that size, even if there's no chance you'll ever give away more than $5.5 million in your lifetime.

Now, if you're a typical middle-class American and you give $20,000 to your grandkid this year, you do have to report that to the government, but what difference does that make? None. All it does is knock $20,000 off your overall $5.5 million exclusion. That's why I say some people know just enough to be dangerous. It's not that they have pulled the $14,000 figure out of thin air. That number really does appear in the rules, but it's only a reporting requirement, not a limit over which you pay any sort of tax. If you, the giver, give more than $14,000 to the same person in a single year, as the giver you are supposed to fill out and submit a gift tax return. At the bottom of that return, your total tax due would be zero. And you have to send in that return only if you and your accountant cannot find a legal way to avoid filing it. For example, each half of a married couple can make gifts up to the $14,000 limit before the requirement to file a return kicks in, so a couple could actually combine to give $28,000 to a grandchild before needing to file a gift tax return. And if that grandchild is married, they could designate a portion of the gift for the grandchild and a portion for the spouse of the grandchild. If they did it that way, they wouldn't have to file a gift tax return until their gifts totaled $56,000. I think you get the picture.

And let me be clear on this: the recipient of a lifetime gift or an inheritance should *never* report that gift as income on his own tax return. If any tax is due for gifted funds, it is payable by the giver, not the person who receives the gift. But given how high current exemption levels are, that's not a problem for most people. Just remember: a gift is not income and never belongs on an income tax report. Most accountants will guide you in the right direction on this rule, but more than once, I have seen people mistakenly include gifts from parents as income because they prepare their returns themselves or use nonaccountant tax services. This increases their income tax liability unnecessarily.

Now if you do have a large estate, the reporting limit is a planning opportunity that some people take advantage of. They want to decrease the value of their estate through gifting over a period of years to minimize or eliminate estate taxes when they die, but that plan is helpful only if they make gifts that do not require them to file a gift tax return. If the lifetime gifts are large enough to require a gift tax return, even if the return shows zero tax liability because they have not used up their lifetime gift tax exemption of nearly $5.5 million, all they're doing is reducing their estate tax exemption. Making reportable gifts is no help in reducing eventual estate taxes. So people in this situation will intentionally give just under the limit to several close family members every year for a period of years. Let's say a couple has three children and each of the three children has a spouse and three children. The grandparents could both give nearly $14,000 to each of their three children, to each of the three spouses, and to each of the nine grandchildren. They will have given away almost $420,000 without using a penny of their nearly $11 million exemption limit because each gift was below the reporting limit. And that's just in one year. Engaging in this sort of planning over a ten-year period could allow them to pass on more than $4 million without paying a penny of gift tax or using a dollar of the combined exemption limit.

Remember, the limit is $14,000 per person per year—it's not an aggregate of all gifts for the year. If you have a high net worth, several family members you want to benefit, and don't mind using lifetime gifts to start decreasing the value of your estate over time, you could engage in a gifting program that could get a lot of money out of your name over a period of years.

A slightly more complex twist on this is available to families with small businesses. They eventually want to pass the business on to their children without any concerns about paying gift or estate taxes. They may have an accountant value their business and determine that, say, 1 percent of their business is worth $10,000. So this businessperson might give 1 percent of the business to her son and 1 percent to her daughter this year. She can continue this process over time, and eventually she could give a large percentage of her business to her children without having to turn in a single gift tax return or to use any of her gift tax exclusion. To be a little more comfortable engaging in a plan like this, she might even speak with an attorney about modifying her corporate documents to ensure that she remains in control of the business no matter what percentage of the business she transfers.

Somehow, some people have come to believe that the reason to stay out of probate is to minimize their estate's tax liability. In fact, your estate does not pay taxes simply because it is in probate. Your estate pays taxes if your net worth exceeds the exemption limit (about $5.5 million for an individual and $11 million for a couple) *and* you don't plan in advance to reduce the size of your estate without using up your exemption on reportable gifts.

Now, if you do have a big estate, you absolutely must work
with a team of professionals to plan ahead because the
estate tax is a hefty one. The maximum estate tax rate
is 40 percent. So, again, if you were single, your estate
wouldn't pay tax on the first $5.5 million, but it would have
to give the IRS a big chunk of everything above $5.5 million.

I need to add one final note on the valuation of estates
before leaving this topic. You may believe you are far from
having a taxable estate, but if you own life insurance policies, you need to include the face value of those policies
before reaching that conclusion. If you didn't use any
type of special planning when purchasing your life insurance—in other words, if you purchased the insurance in
your own name—those policies are part of your estate and
count against your estate tax limit. Say you are a widow
with a valuable house and other large financial assets in
the neighborhood of $3 million. You probably wouldn't
expect to have an issue with estate taxes, but the value
of your estate could approach that $5.5 million exclusion
limit if you also own several million dollars' worth of life
insurance. If you do own large life insurance policies, be
sure to include their value when calculating the value
of your estate and making your planning decisions. You
might consider transferring those policies out of your

name to get them out of your estate.

I call the estate and gift taxes red herrings because these taxes should be the last thing most families should think about when they engage in estate planning. Most families are never going to have more than $11 million to give away in their lifetimes, and they're not going to pass $11 million to their beneficiaries at death. These taxes should not be a focus of their estate planning. In fact, most people should be careful about giving away assets—not because of the gift tax but because of the potentially disastrous effects those gifts can have in relation to the capital gains tax, which I discuss in chapter 5. Others should be careful about gifting because the timing of their gifts could affect their ability to qualify for long-term care benefits, which I discuss in part 3. Still others should think back to the lessons of part 1 and avoid gifting because their would-be beneficiaries are not ready to manage the assets in question. It is important to think about all three strands of planning when considering lifetime gifts and to weigh the potential benefits against the potential pitfalls I warn about throughout this book. Gifting may not be a good idea, even if those gifts are of no interest to the IRS.

This discussion of the estate and gift taxes is related to the first strand of planning in another way, too: trust drafting. Many trusts include special provisions to make sure that a married couple uses the spouses' combined exemptions instead of accidentally using only one. Some will refer to such provisions as credit shelter provisions or A-B provisions. Some call a trust containing these provisions an A-B trust. These are simply trust provisions used by married couples to pass on more assets without having to worry about the estate tax.

Consider, for example, a couple with a large estate, say $8 million. Although this couple has an estate that is much larger than average, they shouldn't have to worry about estate taxes because the estate is still less than the combined exemption limit of $11 million for a married couple. But they could have a problem. What if they own their home and most of their assets jointly and they have named each other as the direct death beneficiary on their retirement accounts and their life insurance? When the first spouse dies, everything is set to go from one spouse directly to the other without probate.

In many respects this is probably exactly what this couple wanted to happen, but without additional planning, it could result in surprise taxation. Let's say the husband dies first, so everything passes directly to the surviving spouse without probate and without any concerns about the estate tax. When an inheritance passes from one spouse to the other, there is never an estate tax, no matter how great their assets. However, when all these assets pass directly from the husband to the wife at the husband's death, the deceased may have failed to use his inheritance tax exemption. Now the surviving spouse is single and has an $8 million estate but only $5.5 million in estate tax exemptions. When the survivor dies, the estate could wind up owing estate taxes on $2.5 million.

In essence, this couple wasted the husband's inheritance tax exemption because everything went directly to the widow and inflated her net worth. While he was still alive, each spouse essentially had a $4 million estate; both estates were well below the limit. But because everything passed to the surviving spouse, she had an $8 million estate when she died, putting her over the estate tax exemption limit, so a large portion of her estate will be subject to estate taxes.

Thanks to some recent changes to the Internal Revenue Code, there's more than one way to avoid this unfortunate outcome, and it occurs much less often than it used to. But the safest and most common way to make sure it doesn't happen is by using a trust with credit shelter provisions, the A-B trust. An A-B trust basically splits your trust into two shares when the first spouse dies. Let's say the husband dies first. Shortly after his death, the trust would be split into an A share and a B share. The wife controls share A as trustee. She is also the beneficiary of share A without restriction. She can serve as trustee and may be the beneficiary of share B as well. Often the only difference is that share B includes some magic language from the tax code that allows the assets passing through that share of the trust to use up the husband's estate tax exemption and keeps those assets out of the final estate of the wife for purposes of calculating her estate taxes. More specifically, share B is written so that the assets can be used only by the trustee (usually the wife) if she determines that the beneficiary (usually also the wife) needs those assets for her health, education, maintenance, or support. Share A contains no such restriction—she can use share A for any purpose.

Did you catch that? To satisfy the IRS and use the husband's estate tax exemption, share B contains a restriction that really isn't much of a restriction. Some sophisticated clients of mine have gotten hung up on the credit shelter language and nearly backed out of trust planning entirely, until they understood that the split between the A share and the B share makes no practical difference at all. It's just a legal distinction that really is important only to the IRS. Establishing an A-B trust does not mean I'm going to give some assets to my wife and some to my kids to deflate her estate artificially. No, that's not what the A-B trust does. Everything can pass from the husband to the wife for the sole benefit of the wife and under the sole control of the wife, if that's what the couple wants. It is hard to see any downside to including such terms in a trust, but they could prove helpful, so it is common to include them as a safety net even if the couple's estate seems unlikely to so much as flirt with taxation even without using both spouses' exemptions.

The estate tax, the gift tax—for most planners they're red herrings. Go ahead and include credit shelter provisions in your trust (I usually do), but do not get bogged down in the technicalities of the provisions, because you'll probably never use them. It's wise to include some basic protective language in your trust because who knows when the estate tax exemption limit might go down or the size of your estate might go way up?

But don't spend a lot of money or mental energy on the estate and gift taxes; there are more important things to worry about. I have reviewed many complicated trusts prepared by prestigious firms with lengthy provisions to minimize estate taxes—for families with a grand total of $300,000 in assets. And too often those same trusts include nothing to protect beneficiaries from creditors, lawsuits, and divorcing spouses.

I also need to stress that I've been talking about the *federal* estate tax. Fourteen states and the District of Columbia levy their own estate tax.[†] The amount varies drastically from state to state. Many apply the tax only to estates worth more than $1 million, but New Jersey's estate tax applies to estates of $675,000 or more. If you live in a state that has an estate tax of its own, you might not be able to rely on the federal government's limit of $5.5 million. That's why you need competent professionals *who practice in your state* to tell you what your state's rules are; a book like this can cover only the general rules and is no substitute for experienced local counsel.

Here's the takeaway: Don't completely ignore estate and gift tax rules, but don't follow the red herring, either. Don't focus your estate planning on issues that are unlikely to ever be issues, especially if that focus causes you to ignore the other planning considerations I discussed in part 1 and will cover in subsequent chapters.

But even though you now know that the estate and gift taxes are not the big deals you thought they were, and you understand that money given to your children during your lifetime or at your death should not be reported on their income tax returns, you can't ignore taxes altogether. What most middle-class families should worry about but often overlook is capital gains taxes, especially those that can be avoided by not succumbing to the desire to *do something now*, like deeding the house to the kids without first consulting an estate-planning attorney. In the next chapter, I explain why capital gains taxes probably deserve more attention during estate planning than any other type of tax.

---

† As of this writing, the states that levy an estate tax are Connecticut, Delaware, Hawaii, Illinois, Maine, Maryland, Massachusetts, Minnesota, New Jersey, New York, Oregon, Rhode Island, Vermont, Washington, and the District of Columbia.

CHAPTER FIVE

Capital Gains Taxes: The Monster Under the Bed

Even though their estate ended up in probate, my grandparents actually did avoid a major problem that befalls a lot of other families. As I discussed in the introduction, my grandparents had set up a trust, which was smart, but they didn't fund the trust. That was bad. So too was missing out on the government benefits for which they were eligible.

What they did right, though, was actually something they

did *not* do. Unlike many people of their generation, my grandparents did not deed their home and their rental property to their children. Many people think that the best, or at least the simplest, way to stay out of probate court is to simply transfer their property to their children now. In part 1, I discussed several reasons why direct gifts to children can be unwise. For one, there's the gremlin problem: the kids might not be ready to own your property. Beyond that, direct gifts, even to mature and responsible children, can open your estate to all sorts of unnecessary legal risks. In part 3, I will discuss the negative consequences that direct gifts can have in the context of long-term care planning. But for my family, capital gains taxes were the biggest reason that direct gifts of my grandparents' home and rental property would have been a problem. The capital gains tax is the tax you pay on the profit you make when you sell real estate, stocks, and other property that can appreciate.

These were not expensive houses. My grandparents lived in a rundown part of Little Rock. Both their home and their rental property were probably worth about $70,000. But they had owned those houses for many, many years. They built their house themselves shortly after they were married, so it would have been difficult to determine its cost so many years later, but for purposes of this discussion, let's assume it cost them $20,000 to build it back in 1944. They bought what became the rental house for $30,000 when my dad was in high school.

Had they proceeded like many people of their generation, late in their lives they would have deeded their properties to their children. That would have addressed the first strand of planning by keeping the family out of probate court. But if my grandparents had used that planning strategy, my dad and his siblings would have spent significantly more money on capital gains taxes than probate costs.

Let's assume my grandparents had deeded their house to my dad. If he sold it shortly after their deaths, when it was still worth about $70,000, he would have had to pay capital gains taxes on the difference between that sale price and my grandparents' cost basis of $20,000. That would have been a taxable profit of $50,000. For most taxpayers, the capital gains tax is 15 percent, so my dad would have had to pay $7,500 in capital gains taxes when he sold my grandparents' home.

Let's assume that my grandparents had deeded their rental house to my aunt. Given its original cost of $30,000, if she sold it shortly after my grandparents' deaths, when it was worth about $70,000, she would have had to pay capital gains taxes of about $6,000 on the $40,000 profit she made.

The lesson here is that when you transfer property to someone as a lifetime gift, the recipient takes on the tax basis of the person who made the transfer. The IRS calls this a carryover basis, because the transferor's tax basis carries over to the transferee in the case of lifetime gifts. This rule applies not only to real estate but also to stocks and any other asset that appreciates over time. In my grandparents' case, the carryover basis rule would have resulted in unnecessary capital gains taxes of $13,500, a cost far greater than what their children incurred in probate court. Thinking only about strand 1, avoiding probate, would have caused even worse problems with strand 2, taxes.

But my grandparents didn't deed their property that way. They made a smart decision in allowing their children to inherit the property after my grandparents died. They intended to pass on their assets through the use of a trust, which would have been better, but even though their estate had to go through probate, at least the method of transfer did not result in unnecessary capital gains taxes. You see, when you inherit property, whether through a trust or probate, as a result of the death of another person, you get what's called a stepped-up tax basis.

Instead of getting stuck with the tax basis of the former owner, you get a new tax basis, what the property was worth on the date of death or, in my grandparents' case, the date of the second spouse's death. My grandfather died first and my grandmother died some years later, so the tax basis of both properties would have been their fair market value on the date of my grandmother's death. Because each property was worth about $70,000 when my grandmother died, and because my dad and his sister sold the properties for something close to that value after they inherited them, they had zero tax liability because their new basis meant there was no taxable gain or profit.

That is why I say that estate and gift taxes are red herrings. The real reason most people should avoid lifetime gifts is the importance of managing their tax basis, so their heirs don't have to send a big fat check to the IRS when they sell the property.

Understand that your heirs won't pay capital gains taxes simply because they received property that appreciated. Capital gains taxes do not come due until your beneficiaries sell the property. The tax on capital gains is a tax on the profit generated by the sale, not a tax on receiving property, whether by gift or inheritance. If you keep this rule in mind, you may be able to minimize or even eliminate capital gains taxes, even if you receive property in a way that gives you an unfavorably low basis.

Say, for example, that my aunt received my grandparents' rental house as a lifetime gift, but she didn't sell it right away. Although my grandparents' low basis of $30,000 would have initially carried over to my aunt, she would have been able to change that basis before selling the property. Suppose she spent $8,000 to add a second bathroom, $7,000 on a kitchen renovation, and $5,000 for a new roof—and those are just the big items. That's $20,000 right there, so my aunt's adjusted basis would actually be $50,000, not the original carryover basis of $30,000 she received. If she then has to pay Realtor fees and closing costs when the property sells, she can deduct those costs—say, $10,000—from her profit, reducing her capital gains to only $10,000 (the $70,000 sale price – the new $60,000 basis) and her tax on the sale to about $1,500 (15 percent of her $10,000 profit). Of course, if she put that much into the property before selling it, she would probably hope to get more than $70,000 for the house. You have to keep that in mind when estimating capital gains taxes.

Taking this lesson one step further, if you receive property with what would be a low carryover basis (your parents' original purchase price) but can prove that your parents spent a lot of money on the property after they bought it but before they gifted it to you, you might be able to establish a higher tax basis because of their expenditures, not just your own. You might have to dig through old records to find bank statements, canceled checks, invoices, or receipts as proof of the improvements they made and what they cost, but the effort could be worth it.

If you don't mind moving, there's another creative way to eliminate capital gains taxes, even if you inherit real estate with a low tax basis. If your parents deed you a house that could cost you a lot of money in capital gains taxes if you sell it, you could consider moving into that house and making it your home for at least two years. In that case, you would receive your own capital gains tax exclusion applicable to the sale of a homestead. If you are single, you can eventually make as much as $250,000 in profit before paying capital gains taxes, and the ceiling on profit for a married couple is $500,000. In the best of all possible worlds, you'll have lived in your own home for at least two years before you sell it to move into your parents' former residence, so you can also use the homestead exclusion when you sell your first house and then use the same exclusion when you sell your parents' former home.

The capital gains tax can pose a huge problem for old family property when the third strand of planning—long-term care—enters the picture. I remember a client who came to see me because her mother was in poor health and in need of assisted living. The daughter told me, "Mom doesn't have money in the bank to pay for something like this. She gets only about $2,000 a month, and that's not going to cover it. All she has is this old family land that she inherited."

"All right," I said. "What is it?"

"It's just forty acres of old family land."

"How long has she had it?" I asked.

"She got it from her mom, who got it from her mom. It's been in the family forever."

I said, "Well, she might be a candidate for some emergency planning. We could gift that property to you in order to get it out of her name so that we can look at long-term care benefits like veterans' benefits or Medicaid."

"Um," she said. "I think I need to talk to my accountant about that first."

"Why is that?" I asked.

"Well, it's actually—according to some Realtors I've talked to—it's worth about $1.5 million now."

It turned out that the property was right in the middle of town in a fast-growing community. When her mother became the owner, the area was little more than a cross-roads, with only a service station and an old pizza joint. Back then, a forty-acre parcel wasn't worth all that much. In fact, the land was appraised at only about $1,000 an acre when she became the owner.

In the years since, the area became heavily developed. Many new neighborhoods popped up, along with restaurants and commercial developments to serve all the new residents in the area. This aging client's property was now highly desirable; it was going to command a high price. So my client was right—I couldn't just transfer it from mother to daughter to reduce my client's asset level for long-term care benefits without giving the daughter a highly unfavorable capital gains tax basis. But she also couldn't simply sell the property to pay for her mother's care without incurring a huge tax bill. She was land rich but cash poor and felt like she was out of decent options.

The plan I used in this case is a great example of how all three strands of planning can intersect. My client's first priority was finding a way to pay for her mother's long-term care, the third strand of planning. Her mother was a great candidate for veterans' benefits now (her late husband was a veteran) and Medicaid down the road but only if I could get this real estate out of her mother's name in an acceptable way. My client wisely noted a second priority, avoidance of unnecessary taxation, the second strand of planning. I had to keep tax basis in mind with any plan I proposed. Against these seemingly contradictory goals, the daughter and I also discussed the first strand of planning, keeping the property out of probate when her mother died.

As it turned out, a specially drafted irrevocable trust met all three goals. First, after proper funding, this trust would keep the mother's estate out of probate court, as would any type of trust. Second, this trust included special terms designed to give the daughter a stepped-up tax basis when she inherited it at her mother's death. Perhaps you are thinking that the stepped-up basis should have been automatic, given that inheritances receive a step up in tax basis, whereas lifetime gifts do not. But many irrevocable trusts are treated like lifetime gifts for tax purposes. It took some special drafting to get my client the basis protection she needed, but it worked out great. Third, because this trust was irrevocable and the mother agreed that I could name her daughter as sole trustee and beneficiary of the trust, leaving the mother out of all roles other than grantor, this trust helped her to qualify for veterans' benefits right away, giving her enough income to pay for assisted living out of pocket. It also helped her prepare for Medicaid in the future, with the five-year lookback applicable to this type of transfer. Three strands of planning, three important goals, and one trust.

Just to recap: Estate and gift taxes were irrelevant in this case because the property, while valuable, was not worth anywhere near $5.5 million. The transfer of such valuable real property was certainly reportable, but this was the mother's only significant asset. She wasn't going to be making any large gifts in the future, and the size of this gift was not going to cause gift tax liability. Reducing her ultimate estate tax exemption at death also was not a consideration. The only tax issue that figured in this plan was the capital gains tax.

Now, if the mother had sold her forty acres herself, she would have had to pay the capital gains taxes. Her basis was $40,000; because the land was vacant, she had no improvements to reduce the amount of profit, which could have been nearly $1.5 million, resulting in a horrific capital gains tax of $225,000. Because she used a trust to transfer this property at death to her daughter, the mother basically eliminated years of appreciation from consideration by the IRS and saved many thousands of dollars in taxes.

That's a strategy to consider when someone late in life is deciding whether to sell property, even if it's not valued in the millions. Some people want to simplify things—"I'm just going to sell my home, my rental house, my acreage, everything. I want to make things simple for my kids." Well, let's figure out how much you're going to pay in capital gains taxes if you sell all those assets compared to what your kids would pay if they sold the property after your death. Maybe the better approach would be to pass the property on to your heirs through a trust so they can get a stepped-up tax basis and eliminate most, if not all, capital gains taxes.

Capital gains taxes should play a prominent role in most people's estate planning, especially when the estate consists of real estate, stocks, and other assets that have appreciated over time, yet this is one of the most overlooked considerations. If you jump the gun and transfer property to your heirs while you're living instead of passing it on as an inheritance upon your death, chances are you are giving them a Trojan horse—and out of it will come not heavily armed soldiers but IRS agents with briefcases and calculators. Everybody loves to find legal ways to beat the system, especially the tax system. I'm not sure there's any better way to beat the tax system than with the lessons in this chapter.

The next chapter is not so much about avoiding taxes as it is about delaying them as long as possible, which is another goal most of my clients share. In chapter 6, I take on the confusing topic of individual retirement accounts and other tax-qualified accounts. The problem with IRAs is that they contain money that has never been taxed. When you take money from your IRA during retirement, you pay income taxes on that money. If you're not careful when passing on your IRA to your heirs, they could end up owing a boatload of income taxes.

CHAPTER SIX

Income Taxes: The Problem with IRAs

A recent client of mine had a small estate but a big problem: the bulk of her estate consisted of an IRA, and her only heir was in no position to receive it. The woman had a house, a small checking account, and a $150,000 IRA. With the help of her financial adviser, she had arranged for it to go to her son upon her death through a direct death beneficiary designation on the account. She was in her second marriage, and she and her husband had separate assets that each intended to leave to their own children.

But she was worried because her only child had recently

filed for bankruptcy. He also was in a rocky marriage that she didn't expect to last. It wasn't that he had an alcohol or drug problem, something we sometimes hear from clients. He just had a really unstable financial history and perhaps an equally fraught future.

The client said she had made her IRA payable directly to her son upon her death because her financial adviser had told her that was the only way to prevent his having to pay all the taxes on that inheritance the minute he receives it. The adviser also told her that was the only way to avoid probate with an IRA. So that was what she did, and it had been set up that way for quite some time.

She said she'd been losing sleep, because she was sure her son would cash the whole thing out the moment he inherited it and would have to pay a ton of taxes despite her planning. She also worried that he would have creditors all over him the second he inherited that money. And she was pretty certain his wife would divorce him and take half of whatever was left. So even though she had followed her financial adviser's advice, she was nonetheless terribly worried that she was putting her son, and his inheritance, in a bad position.

The financial adviser was right to warn that IRAs are subject to special rules because the funds in those types of accounts have never been taxed. Anything she pulled out of the IRA while she was living was subject to regular income tax, and if she wasn't careful, the entire account could indeed have been taxable against her son as soon as he inherited it. The financial adviser was also right to suggest she take action to keep her IRA out of probate court. But he was wrong to suggest that a direct beneficiary designation was the solution in this particular situation. My client was right to be concerned.

The way she set things up, her son could have cashed the IRA as soon as he submitted the death certificate to whichever financial institution held the IRA, and he would have been taxed heavily. Nothing says the beneficiary of an IRA has to roll it over into an IRA in their own name, although that's what a parent hopes will happen when she names her child as the direct beneficiary since that will maintain the tax deferral. The child receives notification from the repository institution that basically says, "You are the beneficiary on your parent's IRA. What would you like us to do with the funds?" If the beneficiary asks for the money, the repository will cut a check. And beneficiaries who don't know the ramifications of that decision will be in for a big surprise when they receive a fraction of the funds they expected because of tax withholdings. In my client's case, even if her son didn't cash out the IRA as soon as it became his property, it would have been subject to all his legal troubles. No wonder my client couldn't sleep at night.

At least in this client's case, she still had time to take action to avoid the consequences that so worried her. I've visited with widows who had been named as direct death beneficiaries of their husbands' IRAs, but because they knew little of their husbands' finances, had poor understanding of IRAs, and received insufficient guidance from the financial institutions involved, these women made really unfortunate mistakes in managing the transition of those funds. They received beneficiary claim forms with two boxes to choose from, one requesting a check and the other initiating a rollover to a survivor IRA. A check sounded pretty good to them, so they marked that box. Then they received checks that were only two-thirds of what they expected. I had a client who thought her husband's IRA had $75,000 in it, and she called me wanting to sue because she got a check for only $50,000. She wanted to know who took her money and was certain something illegal had happened. A quick review of the paperwork showed that the bank had withheld $25,000 for taxes, which was completely appropriate based on the elections she made on the claim form. Under the circumstances, my firm could do nothing to help her by the time she contacted us.

When you use direct beneficiary designations to pass on your IRA, in most cases, your beneficiaries do have the option to either take the money (after taxes are withheld) or roll it into a survivor's IRA. If they don't have the knowledge or sophistication to make the right selection, they might saddle themselves with an unnecessary tax bill, even if they didn't need the money and would have rolled the funds over if they had understood how IRAs worked. Passing on IRAs in this way comes with several downsides, some resulting from a desperate need for money, coupled with bad money management skills, and others from simple ignorance of the rules.

Having a personal relationship with a financial adviser can help with the ignorance part. When you die and it's time to notify your heirs of the funds they are in line to inherit, you don't want them to simply receive blank claim forms in the mail that they won't understand. You want them to get a phone call, a letter, or a visit from the person who has been managing your account for years and can educate them about their options and assist in the whole process.

Unfortunately, having a long-term financial adviser probably wasn't going to help my client. Although her son probably was ignorant of the rules governing IRAs, she feared that, even if he knew the rules, he would cash out because he needed money or was under pressure from his wife. My client also feared his creditors would be standing in line as soon as he had a little bit of money. She would have liked to have named a trustee to manage her IRA for her son, an option I addressed in chapter 3. Even though she didn't call it that, she recognized the gremlin problem. She knew her IRA could turn into a curse for her son, but she was relying on incorrect information from her financial adviser, who had said that the direct beneficiary designation was the only option for handing down her IRA.

The financial adviser wasn't completely wrong—letting an IRA go through probate is a horrible idea. And putting it through a standard trust can absolutely have adverse tax consequences. But he was wrong in thinking that the only alternative was to name her son as the direct beneficiary. There is a better way.

Now, as I've said before, income tax is not usually a big concern in estate planning. Most assets you might inherit are not subject to income taxes; no matter how you receive them, they shouldn't go on your income tax return. If you receive money from a certificate of deposit or a money market or a regular savings account, even if you inherit land and investment accounts, you won't have to pay income taxes. You may have to watch out for capital gains taxes if you sell an asset such as real estate and stocks where basis can be an issue. But you won't pay ordinary income taxes. So, generally speaking, income taxes should not be a concern in your estate planning, except in this one limited area: IRAs and other similar retirement accounts.

The problems with passing on IRAs stem from the very definition of what they are. An IRA is an individual retirement account. A traditional IRA is an account full of money that has never been taxed. As the owner worked, she set aside pretax dollars. Those IRA contributions lowered her current tax obligation because she funneled into this special account some of her income that would have been taxed otherwise. It even grows tax free, so that if it's invested and the markets do well, the interest or dividends it earns are not taxed. This is true not just of IRAs but of any other tax-deferred retirement account, such as a 401(k), a simplified employee pension (SEP), or a 403(b) (a tax-sheltered annuity plan for certain employees of public schools, employees of certain tax-exempt organizations, and certain ministers). These accounts have a variety of names, but the concerns are the same for tax-deferred accounts of any sort, that is, any account funded with pretax dollars.

You are not expected to draw money from a regular IRA before you turn fifty-nine and a half. It is legal to make a withdrawal at any age, but if you withdraw funds early, you have to pay taxes on what you drew out, plus a 10 percent penalty. Of course, you're always going to pay income taxes when you draw from an IRA, no matter what your age, but the 10 percent penalty applies only if you withdraw funds early. Other tax-deferred accounts have similar restrictions. There are some limited exceptions to the penalty for early withdrawals, but they are very restrictive and strictly enforced by the IRS.

Roth IRAs are a little different. A Roth IRA is funded with after-tax dollars; in other words, you do pay taxes on the money that goes into this type of retirement account. But once it's in there, you still don't pay any tax on the growth. Then, on the back end, your withdrawals are not taxable income. So using a Roth IRA doesn't help to decrease income tax liability while you are contributing to the fund, but it's nice not to have to pay taxes on withdrawals down the road.

Let's say that you have a salary of $50,000 a year and you are nowhere near fifty-nine and a half. You take money from your regular IRA because you're having trouble making your car payment. Let's say you take out $10,000 during the year. So when it's time to figure your taxes for that year, it's as if you made $60,000 that year—your $50,000 salary plus the $10,000 you took out of this retirement account. You're also going to pay a 10 percent penalty because you put the money in an IRA but didn't leave it there long enough. Making car payments isn't one of those permissible exceptions.

When you hit the magic age of fifty-nine and a half, the rule changes. You can draw money out of your IRA whenever you want without penalty, but that doesn't mean you can draw it out without paying taxes on it. The 10 percent penalty is gone, but you still pay taxes on what you withdrew at whatever tax rate applies to your income, just as if you had earned that money in the year you drew it out.

Now, when you reach seventy and a half, the rules change again. By that age, you *have* to start withdrawing funds from an IRA at least once a year. There's something called a required minimum distribution, or RMD. You have to withdraw an amount determined by formulas published by the IRS. Essentially, the government is saying, "We let you put this money in tax free, and we let it grow tax free, but you can't leave it there forever." The idea is that when you have to start taking RMDs, you will be in a lower tax bracket than you were in your working years, so the tax hit won't be as bad. When you inherit an IRA, there is no penalty for withdrawals, no matter your age, but you still have to pay taxes on all withdrawals from an inherited IRA, and in most cases, you have to take RMDs starting in the first year you inherit the money, no matter how old you are.

Even though you have to start taking RMDs right away when you inherit an IRA, your life expectancy is behind the IRS formula for calculating the amount. If you are younger than the person from whom you inherited the IRA, your RMDs will be smaller than those for the creator of the IRA if that person was older than seventy and a half at death. If you are much younger, your RMDs will be much smaller. With proper management and good decision making, you can defer the taxes on the funds in an IRA and their past and future growth for a long time. And who wants to pay taxes before you have to?

When it comes to estate planning for IRAs, you must keep these main goals in mind:

1. Ensuring your IRA doesn't wind up in probate. That's a given with any type of asset.
2. Ensuring taxes are stretched for as long as legally possible—you want to avoid doing anything that might result in immediate taxation of the funds upon your death.
3. Protecting your IRA beneficiaries from themselves if they're young, unsophisticated, or bad with money and protecting them from others, if they have legal problems that might put their inheritance at risk.

Basic estate planning can easily address any two of these concerns but not all three. The simplest way to pass on a retirement account at death is through a direct beneficiary designation on the account itself. That keeps the account out of probate, and it will give the beneficiaries the ability to continue the tax deferral through their own life expectancies if they are wise enough to roll the money into a survivor IRA. But a direct beneficiary designation does nothing to protect the funds from the creditors of the beneficiaries or from a divorce settlement, nor does it protect the money from the bad judgment of the beneficiaries.

On the other hand, you could name as the death beneficiary of your IRA the trust you established to keep your house and other nonretirement assets out of probate. This planning strategy also keeps the IRA out of probate. And with a properly drafted trust (see chapter 3), you can protect your heirs' inheritance from their creditors, potential ex-spouses, and other legal problems. Other provisions could protect the heirs from their own poor money management. So, again, this planning option meets two of the three planning goals.

The downside of naming a typical trust as the death beneficiary of an IRA is that the ultimate recipients must pay all taxes on the funds within five years of inheritance; they cannot defer the taxes the way they could with a direct beneficiary designation. This can be a huge financial hit, and it is what makes most financial advisers say you cannot name a trust as beneficiary of an IRA.

A third option is available when it comes to estate planning with IRAs—one that can meet all three goals at the same time. You could name a special type of trust—an IRA trust—as the death beneficiary of your retirement account.

The IRA trust will keep your IRA out of probate, preserve the tax-deferred nature of the account just like a direct death beneficiary would have, and protect the beneficiaries from bad decisions and from others who would try to get some of that money.

The IRA trust offers a couple of other, often overlooked, benefits as well. If you have a disabled child who would lose disability or Medicaid benefits if you left your IRA directly to that child, you can set up an IRA trust with special needs trust provisions to preserve that child's eligibility for benefits, just like you might have done in a typical revocable trust.

You can also use an IRA trust to protect minor children who aren't old enough to inherit an IRA. In fact, passing an IRA to a young child through an IRA trust can be one of the most advantageous uses of this type of trust, since the RMDs are much lower for younger beneficiaries. Imagine the almost tax-free growth of a well-funded IRA with RMDs based on the life expectancy of a ten-year-old but managed by a sophisticated adult. It doesn't get much better than that. As I'm writing this, my children are seven and ten, legally too young to inherit an IRA. But I'm still not comfortable with the idea of giving my IRA directly to them even at eighteen when they are no longer minors. I want them to wait until they're thirty before they have direct control of my IRA. With an IRA trust, I can leave the money for their benefit at any age if my trustee deems the use to be appropriate while also specifying how old they must be before they have direct control of the funds.

I know this sounds similar to the discussion in chapter 3, but I can't stress enough that you cannot use a typical trust to do these things with IRAs. You must use an IRA trust to preserve the tax-deferred nature of the accounts. Many people will set up an IRA trust as a companion to a standard revocable trust, funding the revocable trust with their house and nonretirement assets while naming the IRA trust as the beneficiary for all retirement accounts. The terms of the two trusts can be essentially the same, with the exception of the special terms the IRS requires for the IRA trust in order to maintain the tax deferrals. Or you can set up the two trusts with very different terms. For example, you could leave the assets in your revocable trust to your children while naming your grandchildren as beneficiaries of the IRA trust, with your children as trustees for the protection of the grandchildren.

To protect minor children or grandchildren, disabled beneficiaries, or older children who cannot be trusted to manage the IRA properly, the IRA trust puts a trusted individual in charge of the funds, the way Ted Kennedy handled his estate. You can, of course, use a corporate fiduciary, such as the trust department of a bank or a financial institution. The costs and fees would be similar to what they charge to manage any other kind of trust. Or you can name a friend or family member as trustee, who may or may not charge a fee. If you are not worried about protecting older beneficiaries from themselves and their own bad decisions, you can allow them to serve as trustee of the IRA trust, which will still protect them from outside threats.

One other benefit of an IRA trust is something that no one wants to think about: the possibility that a child could predecease you. That possibility makes use of an IRA trust advisable, even if you have adult children who are financially responsible. If nothing unexpected happens, your responsible, low-risk children will receive your IRA through the direct beneficiary designation with no adverse consequences. But the premature death of a child could mean one of two undesirable outcomes for your IRA. It could result in a probate, if you named no alternate beneficiary in the event a primary beneficiary dies. Or it could mean the IRA passes directly to a beneficiary who is not as responsible and low risk as the deceased child was. For example, you might have named the children of the deceased child as alternate beneficiaries without thinking about their stage in life when they receive those funds. You could also run into the problem Marilyn Monroe's estate faced if your child dies after inheriting your IRA—he might have redirected it to someone you didn't intend to have it.

An IRA trust is written in a way that plans for all sorts of contingencies. An IRA trust will say, "I leave this money to my three kids, but if any have died before I do, leave the money in equal shares to my surviving children." Or, "Let the share of any deceased child pass down to my grandchildren—that is, the children of my deceased child, but do not give them direct control of the funds until they reach the age of thirty." You could include almost any instruction you want for all possible contingencies.

I proposed an IRA trust to the client who was losing sleep because of her concerns about her son's ability to manage her IRA and what she saw as a probable divorce in his future. She, like a lot of people, ended up doing two trusts. She and her husband set up one trust; it contained their home and vehicles, personal property, and modest non-retirement financial accounts, and it split those assets between his children and her child. Then she set up an IRA trust of her own to receive and protect her IRA funds at her death. In both trusts, she built in protections for her son, and she and her husband were able to divide their assets between their families just as they had always intended.

When it comes to tax issues in estate planning, the bottom line is this: for most families, estate and gift taxes will be nonissues; for almost all estates, at least all estates that contain real estate and stocks, capital gains taxes can be a huge issue; and income taxes will be an issue only for those estates that contain IRAs and other retirement funds. For estates that do not include retirement funds of any kind, income taxes may be as much a nonstarter as the estate tax.

I don't mean to suggest that every family with an IRA is going to need an IRA trust. But there is no magic formula for determining when an IRA warrants trust planning. In my case, considering the young ages of my children, even a small IRA should be payable to an IRA trust. The same thing is true for the IRA of a parent seeking to take care of a disabled child of any age—even a small IRA will disqualify that child from receiving essential government benefits. But for families with older children who are not disabled, deciding whether to establish an IRA trust means weighing the need for protection and the value of the tax deferrals against the cost of preparing such a trust.

My purpose here has been simply to point out various situations in which using an IRA trust is a smart thing to do so that you can make a considered decision about whether you need to have one. It's definitely worth spending half an hour with your financial adviser and consulting with your attorney to discuss your beneficiaries and their particular circumstances. Even if you decide not to use an IRA trust, make sure you ask your financial adviser exactly what will happen with your IRA when you die based on the paperwork you've already signed and adjust your direct beneficiary designations if appropriate.

This concludes my discussion of the first two of the three strands of planning, and I hope you have seen how interconnected the first and second strands of planning really are. You read about several perfectly legal ways to transfer assets to your heirs outside probate that would mean horrible capital gains tax consequences for them. You have learned how use of a revocable trust can be an excellent way to protect your heirs and their inheritance of anything except an IRA. If you focus on strand 1 while ignoring the tax issues important to consider with strand 2, you can plan yourself into disastrous consequences— sometimes causing worse problems than you solved with your planning.

You will find the same to be true with the third strand—

long-term care planning. In part 3, I will teach you how some of the most common estate-planning techniques designed to address the concerns of strand 1 (staying out of probate) can backfire when it comes to paying for long-term care. I will also show you how some common techniques for planning for long-term care can have adverse tax consequences. The discussion of planning for long-term care begins in chapter 7.

PART III

The Third Strand: Protecting Your Estate from Long-Term Care Costs

(Or Making Sure There's Something Left to Pass On)

CHAPTER SEVEN

Long-Term Care: How to Pay for It but Not Out of Your Pocket

In no other area of law do I see clients so eager to understand the rules but struggle so mightily to get a good grasp of them. So much incomplete and downright incorrect information is in circulation about long-term care, it's no wonder people are confused. But the need to understand long-term care and how to pay for it is serious. With apologies to Ben Franklin: nothing in this world is certain except death and taxes...and, increasingly, the need for long-term care. And it is expensive.

The average life expectancy in the United States is at an all-time high—about eighty years. The average sixty-five-year-old today is expected to live at least another twenty years but has an almost 70 percent chance of needing long-term care at some point. Men tend to need long-term care for an average of two years; for women, the average is twice as long. But it is not at all uncommon for someone to need long-term care for more than five years.

Nursing homes provide more than a third of long-term care services. The national average for a semiprivate room in a nursing home is about $80,000 a year—and that's with a roommate. A private room is closer to $90,000. For a lower level of care, assisted living facilities have become popular long-term care options. Assisted living is less expensive than nursing home care, but the national average is still more than $40,000 per year. And remember: These costs are per person. When both spouses in a married couple need care, you can be sure the costs will be much higher.

A third long-term care option is the use of caregivers in the home. Nationally, the average pay for a home caregiver is $21 per hour, so the cost of home care can vary more widely than the cost of facility-based care depending on the hours of services needed, but the average annual cost is about $45,000 per year. But not all home care is provided by professionals. According to the AARP Public Policy Institute's June 2015 report, *Caregiving in the U.S.*, an estimated 34.2 million adults in the United States—about 14.3 percent of all adult Americans—gave care to an adult aged fifty or older in the previous twelve months. These are seniors who can't or don't want to pay for long-term care services. About 25 percent of primary caregivers—"those who provide all or the majority of the unpaid care for their recipient"—are caring for immediate family members, and they spend an average of 24.4 hours a week giving that care, the AARP found. Almost 60 percent of these family caregivers "assist with medical/nursing tasks," the AARP reported.

I trust by now that I have your attention and you realize that you can't just hope you won't need long-term care—the odds are against you. And if you bet wrong, your gamble can be really expensive. In fact, it's so expensive that it can quickly wipe out the average person's estate.

You could have the best plan in the world for avoiding probate and minimizing taxes after learning about the first two strands of planning. You've outlined exactly where everything is supposed to go and how it is supposed to get there. No probate. No courts. No lawyers. No judges. Little cost. Little hassle. But if nothing is left because it's all been liquidated to pay for long-term care costs, what did you accomplish? You may make brilliant decisions with regard to capital gains taxes and IRAs, but if you have to cash everything out or sell your house to meet expenses, all that tax planning went to waste. So the third strand of estate planning involves long-term care. If you need it, you will hardly be in an unlucky minority. And failure to plan for long-term care can trump even the best planning for avoiding probate and minimizing taxes.

You can pay for long-term care in four ways: out of your own pocket, by purchasing a long-term care insurance policy in advance of need; by receiving veterans' benefits (for those with qualifying service); or by using Medicaid assistance. In this chapter, I will address the three options for paying for long-term care that are much more desirable than paying out of pocket.

The lessons of this chapter are personal for me. Both of my paternal grandparents had opportunities throughout their later years to draw on veterans' benefits but never did, because they did not know about them. They were unaware such benefits existed, never mind how to apply for them or plan for their eligibility. And Medicaid could have provided my grandmother with much-needed financial assistance to pay for her long-term care while she was confined to a nursing home, but, again, lack of knowledge and lack of planning took that option off the table, too.

My grandparents' escalating long-term care needs were typical—the same progression I see every day in my law practice. When both my grandparents were living and still at home but needed assistance to stay there, their children provided the help they needed. My father and his siblings were helping their parents on a regular, eventually a daily, basis. Although my dad, my aunt, and my uncle all had full-time jobs, they became full-time caregivers as well.

As a World War II veteran, my grandfather would have been an ideal candidate for the veterans' benefit commonly called aid and attendance; it would have reimbursed my grandparents for the cost of hiring someone to provide in-home assistance. That person could have been one of their children, but it also could have been a professional whose efforts would have allowed their children to resume more normal schedules.

After my grandfather died and my grandmother moved in with my aunt and her family, she was a prime candidate for the widow's benefit through the same VA program, which also would have helped pay for her stay when she moved to the assisted living facility, but she never even looked into it. And benefits under the program would have at least defrayed the cost of her nursing home care. That makes four times she missed out on those veterans' benefits. She also missed out on Medicaid assistance for her nursing home care.

My grandparents would never have considered long-term care insurance because of their views about spending money and the limited availability of long-term care policies when they could have qualified medically. But long-term care policies have evolved significantly since then, and they are becoming much more attractive options. In the first part of this chapter, I will address how long-term care insurance works, when to buy it, and what to look out for when selecting a policy. I will then discuss veterans' benefits and long-term care Medicaid programs: what they cover, their income rules, their asset limits, and how to qualify.

LONG-TERM CARE INSURANCE

The first thing to understand about long-term care is that, with the limited exception of policies specifically designated for long-term care, insurance won't pay for it. Medicare, Medicare supplements, and private health insurance do not cover long-term care.

A lot of people think that Medicare covers long-term care expenses. It does not. Medicare is a government health insurance plan. People get confused about what Medicare will pay for because their friends or family members in nursing homes have received limited Medicare coverage for a short-term stay. But that's because the resident was there for rehabilitation. Medicare will pay for inpatient rehabilitation at a nursing home or for outpatient rehab, but only for a limited time. At most, Medicare and a good Medicare supplement will pay for one hundred days of inpatient rehabilitation in a nursing home, but most people get nowhere near one hundred days because the providers determine that such a long stint is not medically appropriate. And rehab providers are quick to terminate Medicare coverage because, if the rehab facility tries to bill Medicare for rehabilitation services provided past the point of benefit, they're going to get into trouble for making improper claims. Overprovision of medical services and overbilling Medicare is a hot issue these days, so when rehab services are no longer appropriate, yes, the nursing home is going to be quick to send you home or move you to long-term care in the facility.

Even for inpatient rehab, you should understand that Medicare doesn't pick up the full tab for the entire stay. Medicare pays in full for a maximum of twenty days of rehab; after twenty days it pays 80 percent of costs up to the hundred-day limit, but for no longer than is medically appropriate. If you have a good Medicare supplement, or secondary insurance, it typically covers all or most of the 20 percent copay for rehabilitation. That's important because a lot of people don't realize that inpatient rehabilitation at a nursing home is so expensive that even a 20 percent copay can run $4,000 to $5,000. Medicare will also pay for outpatient rehabilitation when appropriate, but here, too, Medicare limits the number of days and the amount of services.

Long-term care insurance is a specific type of policy taken out with the express purpose of obtaining coverage to pay for long-term care services. There's no mistaking it—it has a good, clear name. In the insurance world, long-term care insurance is the only insurance that pays for long-term care.

And it's expensive. Annual premiums vary by state and are pegged to the average cost of long-term care in your state. According to the AARP's website, in 2011, a historical sampling of three annual premiums for a sixty-year-old man ranged from $1,945 to $2,877 for coverage of $5,000 a month for five years with no inflation protection and varying other benefits. The organization adds that prices can drop over time: the policy with the highest annual premium came from 2011, but in 2014 "this same coverage on a modern policy (2014) would start at around $2,596/ year." Still, you can't count on a price drop; you probably can count on regular increases.

Suffice it to say that it's expensive. That's why I at least mention long-term care insurance even to young parents;

the sooner they are at least aware of it and start thinking about whether they want it, the better. The younger you are and the better your health is, the less expensive your annual premium for a long-term care policy will be. But *Consumer Reports* had this to say in 2012:

> *You'll pay less if you buy a policy before age 60. A plan that pays $3,000 a month for four years with a 5 percent compound inflation option and a 60-day elimination period might cost $2,815 a year for a 57-year-old healthy male. At 62, the same policy might cost $3,248 a year. "After 60, insurers figure we're like cars; our parts are older, start to break down, and cost more to fix," says Owen Malcolm, a fee-only planner in Norcross, Ga. But if you buy a policy in your 50s you could end up paying premiums—including future price hikes—for decades and never collect any benefits.*

So there's a balancing act here. The earlier you purchase long-term care insurance, the more likely you are to make it through medical underwriting and the lower your premiums will be. The longer you wait, the more likely you may be to have a health event or diagnosis that disqualifies you for coverage, and, if you can obtain coverage at all, your premiums will be higher. But buying it early means paying for it longer.

You also need to know—especially if you have had a policy for some time—that not all policies are created equal. I've seen some long-term care policies that cover only inpatient nursing home care but not assisted living or home care. I've also seen the opposite: some policies that cover only home care and provide no coverage for nursing homes. If the people who purchased those policies had realized how limited they are, they probably would not have paid for them.

I recently met someone who had an older policy, and it covered all long-term care options but not for "illness of the mind." What would that be? Well, that would be dementia, one of the primary reasons people purchase long-term care policies.

The point is that not all policies cover the same things. If you already have one, pull that thing out, call your agent, and be sure you know what you have.

Another point to be aware of is that some policies have what's called an inflation rider (5 percent is considered the gold standard, but 3 percent probably is adequate these days, and it can make a big difference in your premium). It means that as inflation increases the cost of care, your coverage increases. Your premiums probably go up as well.

Some don't have inflation riders. I've had clients tell me, "Oh, I think Mom has long-term care insurance—we should be fine." Well, she took the policy out twenty years ago, and her coverage is $1,000 a month. That's a fraction of what her services will cost. Amounts of coverage vary significantly from one policy to the next. If it's an older policy with an inflation rider, it's probably fine. Older policies without inflation riders may not offer enough coverage considering today's costs.

That said, you don't necessarily have to take out a long-term care insurance policy to cover the entire cost of care. You can expect to use your social security payments or retirement savings to supplement what the insurance policy pays, allowing you to take out a smaller policy with lower premiums. You may want just enough insurance to make up the difference.

Policies also have strict rules about when you get to draw on them, which is another reason to check what you have. Usually, you can draw on your long-term care insurance policy when you need significant assistance with at least two activities of daily living, such as bathing or feeding or dressing. That's a fairly strict standard—you have to be in pretty serious need.

Typically, if your policy covers ailments of the mind, a

diagnosis of dementia in and of itself may make you eligible for coverage under your policy, even if you are physically able to perform the activities of daily living for yourself. If you need regular routine supervision for your protection—because you cannot remember to bathe or eat or get dressed or turn off the stove, or you have to be reminded or helped to do those things—that would trigger coverage under your policy.

If you don't already have a long-term care policy but are looking into it, then be sure to explore all options. What I mean is that a lot of traditional long-term care insurance plans are what you might call use-it-or-lose-it plans, not unlike auto insurance. You pay a monthly or annual premium for the insurance. You draw on it only if something bad happens. You hope that something bad doesn't happen, but if you stay perfectly healthy and capable, your premiums are just gone. Some newer policies you might want to explore include a death benefit rider so that if you don't use your insurance for long-term care needs, the premiums you paid can convert to a death benefit for your family. Sometimes these policies look like life insurance with a long-term care coverage rider. Sometimes they look like long-term care insurance with a life insurance rider. Either way, it's just another variation of long-term care insurance that I think people ought to look into as they decide how they will pay for long-term care.

VA PENSION WITH AID AND ATTENDANCE

Throughout most of this book, I have broadly used the term *veterans' benefits* to refer to a category of benefits that may be available to certain seniors in need of long-term care. In reality, several different types of benefits are available through the VA, and a discussion of only one such benefit belongs in this book. So for the purposes of this chapter, it is not sufficient to broadly discuss "veterans' benefits." The discussion here focuses on the long-term care benefit available through the VA: the VA Pension with Aid and Attendance.

First, you should understand what this benefit is not. The aid and attendance benefit is not a service-connected disability benefit, which is also known as VA compensation. Service-connected disability benefits are for service members who were injured in the line of duty, have a certain disability rating, and are entitled to compensation from the VA as a result of their disability. Service-connected disability has no income or asset limits, and claimants do not have to live in a long-term care facility or receive assistance from home caregivers in order to qualify. That is not the benefit I'm talking about here.

The VA Pension with Aid and Attendance is for older veterans who are now in need of long-term care services because of age or illness, not any type of service-related injury. The aid and attendance benefit is not a health insurance plan that pays a service provider, and it does not require claimants to use VA health-care services. It is tax-free income paid directly to qualifying veterans and, in some cases, their widows; it is meant to reimburse them for long-term care expenses.

Married veterans who qualify for the maximum aid and attendance benefit receive a direct deposit of about $2,100 per month. Single veterans can receive about $1,800 per month, and the surviving spouse of a veteran who qualifies for the benefit can receive about $1,150. Like social security benefits, these figures usually change every year.

The VA has three separate sets of criteria that it uses to determine whether a veteran or a surviving spouse will qualify for the aid and attendance benefit: the veteran's service status, health, and financial need. Claimants must qualify under all three to receive the benefit.

First, the aid and attendance benefit is available only to veterans with a certain service status and the surviving spouses of qualifying veterans. Veterans must submit discharge papers proving that they served on active duty for at least ninety days, any one day of which occurred during a congressionally declared period of war, including World War II, the Vietnam War, the Korean War, and the

Persian Gulf War. The veteran need not have seen combat to qualify, but service in the reserves does not count as active duty service. The veteran's discharge from service can be of any type other than dishonorable.

Second, the aid and attendance benefit is available only to veterans or their surviving spouses when they require long-term care as a result of age or disability. When the problem is physical, the criterion is similar to—but not quite as strict as—that for tapping long-term care insurance: you must need assistance with at least two activities of daily living to qualify. Claimants who are legally blind will automatically satisfy this requirement, as will claimants who reside in a nursing home. When the problem is cognitive, a diagnosis of dementia of any kind will likely satisfy this requirement. Generally, a claimant's personal physician will provide all the evidence needed to satisfy the VA's health requirements. The VA provides a "physician's affidavit" form to be completed by any physician who is familiar with the claimant's health. The VA does not require any sort of examination by a VA health-care provider.

Veterans and surviving spouses older than sixty-five who meet all other requirements for veterans' benefits but do not have a serious medical diagnosis or health problem that requires long-term care assistance may be entitled to a smaller pension under this program.

Third, the aid and attendance benefit is available only to veterans and surviving spouses who have low income and limited assets. But this is where the requirements become significantly more complicated. I have known many veterans who called an 800 number at the VA to ask if they might qualify for "benefits," only to be asked one question: "What's your income?" Regardless of the answer, the person on the other end of the line nearly always says that the caller is not qualified. Now, no one can determine whether a veteran is qualified for the aid and attendance benefit based on that one question, and you'll understand why when I explain the real income test applicable to this benefit.

Before I do that, let me remind you that the surviving spouse of a veteran is often a candidate for this benefit under the same criteria used to determine whether the veteran is qualified. But if you're the surviving spouse of a veteran, you must present additional evidence with your application for benefits. You have to prove you're truly the surviving spouse of that veteran. I once worked on a case for two or three months, visiting my client at her assisted living facility to gather information and to obtain signatures on important paperwork.

"Now, I've been meaning to ask you," she said. "Does it matter that he and I divorced before he died?"

I said, "Yes, ma'am. That does matter. You're not a widow of a veteran if you divorced before he died." So there went months of work. Yes, divorce means you cannot claim to be the widow of a veteran.

Remarriage also disqualifies the widow of a veteran. Say you were married to a veteran for fifty years, and then he died and you remarried and your new husband is not a veteran. You can no longer claim veterans' benefits under this program.

On a few occasions, I've had children bring their older parent and significant other to me for a consultation. The adult child will tell me, "My dad wants to get married. He was married to my mom for fifty years and she died; now he wants to marry his fiancée. She's a great person. I just worry that this is going to cause a lot of problems. What should they be thinking about?"

I usually look at the fiancée and say, "Well, what about you? Were you previously married to a veteran?" If so, by marrying again she's going to cut herself off from benefits to which she might have been entitled.

On the other hand, the aid and attendance benefit may be a reason to get married. The fiancée in that scenario may have a lot of medical expenses but doesn't qualify for any benefits. Maybe her potential spouse is a veteran, but he can't claim the benefits for her unless they get married. In either case, veterans' benefits can play an important role in the decision to marry late in life.

Let me return to the third criterion, financial status. The VA breaks this part of its analysis of a veteran's eligibility into two separate tests: the income test and the asset test. As you might expect, under the income test, the VA looks at your overall income—not just what hits the bank on a monthly basis but also annual income, such as required disbursements from your retirement accounts. The asset test considers everything you own, except for your home and your vehicle. Everything else counts, whether it's in your own name, held jointly with another person, or titled in the name of most types of trusts.

The income test is actually a formula. And it's anything but straightforward—it's extremely confusing. That is why being told by a VA call center that you aren't qualified because your income is too high is no reason to stop looking into the aid and attendance benefit. You cannot look at a chart and decide whether someone qualifies.

To be clear, a chart *is* involved in the determination. Claimants with an "income for VA purposes" that is higher than the award amount for which they are applying fail the income test, so the VA's maximum award levels play a key role in the determination. The trick is to understand the phrase "income for VA purposes," or IVAP.

The formula sounds pretty simple at first: your IVAP is your gross annual income less your qualified recurring medical expenses. That's a term of art: *qualified recurring medical expenses.* For married claimants, the VA considers the gross annual income of both spouses, but it also deducts the qualified recurring medical expenses of both spouses. If your income, using that formula, is zero or a negative number, you qualify for the maximum aid and attendance benefit available to those with your status (married, single, or surviving spouse). To put it another way, if your qualified recurring medical expenses equal or exceed your gross annual income from all sources, you will pass the income test and be in line to receive the full benefit.

This is *not* an all-or-nothing benefit. If someone uses that formula and determines his IVAP is $500, meaning his income exceeds his qualified recurring medical expenses by $500, that's okay. All that means is that the VA is going to subtract $500 from the total benefit he might have received, but he will be approved for the benefit. So if a married claimant seeking the $2,100 –benefit has an IVAP of $500, he will not be denied because his IVAP is greater than zero; he'll be approved for a benefit of about $1,600 per month ($2,100 – $500).

So the formula has two components. Gross annual income means social security benefits, pension benefits, retirement checks, draws you take from your retirement accounts, and any interest you earn on your bank accounts and investments. All those things count as your income. And remember: for married veterans, the VA considers the income of both spouses.

Qualified recurring medical expenses include small things such as health insurance premiums, Medicare premiums, drug plan premiums, and long-term care insurance premiums. The larger qualified recurring medical expenses are fees paid to home caregivers, assisted living facilities, and nursing homes. A big distinction you need to be aware of is that *independent* living is not the same as *assisted* living. It is difficult to convince the VA to include fees paid for independent living as qualified recurring medical expenses, but it routinely includes assisted living fees in that definition.

Home care counts as a qualified recurring medical expense, whether the care is provided by a family member, a professional company, or a neighbor. The key is that you really must be receiving necessary services, and you really must be paying for those services. The caregiver doesn't have to have any sort of special certifications or qualifications. The VA will allow your children to serve as your caregivers. They probably wouldn't have charged you, and you probably wouldn't have expected to pay them, but if you want to qualify for the VA benefit, you must pay for your caregiver services, even if your own family provides them.

As this book went to press, the rules for the asset test were relatively straightforward. There is no set monetary value in any statute or VA rule, but the guidelines most advisers follow say that married veterans will not qualify if they have more than $80,000 in countable assets (excluding the house and car). And for single veterans, the target is $40,000. That's pretty straightforward.

As I write this, the law does not prohibit or penalize the transfer of assets before you apply for the benefits. If you gave away assets in the year before—even the month before—you filed for benefits, that's irrelevant. The application asks only for assets as of the date of application. This is in sharp contrast to the rules relevant to Medicaid coverage, and in the near future, it may no longer be true for the aid and attendance benefit. The VA has proposed a three-year lookback for asset transfers and harsh penalty periods for transfers occurring within that lookback.

A lookback is a window in time before application for assistance that a government agency is permitted to use to look for and then penalize asset transfers.

So as the law stands now, if you're over the asset limit, you can rearrange your assets, perhaps retitling them in one way or another, maybe by using an irrevocable trust to shelter your assets, and you are not doing anything illegal or unethical. Under current VA rules, those transfers are completely permissible.

However, you should be aware that the VA does a sort of an informal lookback that occasionally causes trouble. The VA has the power to compare the information included on your application with your IRS records from previous years, and when that comparison turns up inconsistencies, the VA can hold up an application.

For example, if you had investments with Edward Jones last year that regularly kicked out dividends, your IRS records will show that. This year, that Edward Jones account may be gone—either you spent it all or you sheltered it in an irrevocable trust, but it's gone. Your application for aid and attendance will say nothing about your Edward Jones account because you don't have one anymore. But when the VA matches your application against last year's tax records, it may see the inconsistency as a red flag and ask for an explanation. The VA can extend an application process indefinitely if it is not satisfied with the explanation.

That leads me to a final note about veterans' benefits: The VA is not known for moving quickly—far from it. The department is not as slow as it was a few years ago when it had a huge backlog and veterans died after waiting more than a year for approval from the VA. But it is still common to wait five or six months for the VA to process an application. The good news is, if you are eventually approved for benefits, the VA provides back pay for every month you waited for the approval notice. So if a surviving spouse is approved for the maximum benefit after waiting six months for his application to be processed, he'll receive an award of about $1,150 per month, plus a check for back pay of nearly $7,000.

MEDICAID

Unlike the aid and attendance benefit available through the VA, Medicaid benefits do not pay any funds directly to qualified recipients. Instead, Medicaid operates more like health insurance, paying directly to service providers on behalf of those who are qualified. Medicaid benefits are managed by each state, but they are primarily federally funded.

But before I get into the rules, I want to address a widely held misunderstanding: many people think that if they have to rely on Medicaid to pay for their long-term care, they are doomed to substandard care. That's simply not true. It is illegal for a facility to discriminate against a resident because she or he is covered by Medicaid. In fact, the vast majority of nursing home residents are on Medicaid. The only question is whether they spent all their money on care, went broke, and then got on Medicaid or whether they engaged in some of the planning I discuss later in this book to qualify for Medicaid coverage.

Now, it is true that not every facility accepts Medicaid coverage. Just as some hospitals refuse to accept certain types of insurance, facilities may choose not to participate in the Medicaid program. But the vast majority of nursing homes, and (in Arkansas at least) many assisted living facilities, accept Medicaid, and those facilities that do cannot have lower standards of care for, or provide inferior services to, Medicaid recipients.

But because not every facility accepts Medicaid and not every state has a Medicaid program to cover assisted living and home care, you must put a lot of thought as well as research into whether it is wise for you to count on Medicaid coverage for your long-term care needs. If you have in mind a particular facility that you know does not accept Medicaid, or if your state does not have a Medicaid program for assisted living or home care and those long-term care options are more attractive to you than nursing home care, then you should be much more motivated to purchase long-term care insurance or make sure you can qualify for veterans' benefits.

Now, someone with $500,000 in assets might not want to pursue Medicaid because the planning necessary to make them eligible when the time comes is not appealing to them. If that person tells me, "I would rather just pay for my own care than to have to go through any special legal process to save my money," that's a perfectly valid decision. That person also should be motivated to seriously consider long-term care insurance. But avoiding Medicaid benefits because of a fear of substandard care should not be the determinant.

So what are the rules for Medicaid eligibility? To some extent, they vary by state, but the basic rules for Medicaid eligibility are similar across the country, and they are strict. Qualifying for Medicaid is difficult, but if you do, it's an extremely valuable benefit. As a general rule, Medicaid recipients make a sort of copay to their long-term care facility based on their income, and then Medicaid pays that facility directly for the rest of the amount due based on reimbursement rates negotiated by Medicaid. So if a nursing home resident who is qualified for Medicaid receives only $1,000 per month in social security benefits and no other income, but her facility costs $6,000 per month, she will contribute only a portion of her social security income to the cost of care (something less than $1,000), and Medicaid will cover all other costs.

In all states, Medicaid uses an asset test to determine eligibility for benefits. Some states also have income restrictions, but some have done away with the income limits. Those states have recognized that if you are filing for Medicaid to pay for your care in a facility, the law requires you to pay the bulk of your income toward the cost of care before Medicaid pays the difference. Why make it harder for someone with more income to qualify for Medicaid than a person with less income when neither has sufficient income to cover the entire cost of care and both have to contribute most of their income to the facility anyway? The state will simply pay less on behalf of applicants with more income to contribute to the cost of their care.

If you're in a state like Arkansas, which still has income limits, you need to know what those limits are. The income limit in Arkansas and in several other states right now is about $2,200 a month. You also need to realize that the income limit is based on gross income, before any deductions, not what hits the applicant's bank account after deductions. People always report their social security wrong, because they don't include the Medicare premium that is automatically deducted from social security.

If your gross income is more than the current income limit (in those states that still have income limits), you can set up something called an irrevocable income trust and still qualify for Medicaid benefits. Some refer to this trust more casually as a Miller trust. This is a trust commonly created by a lawyer, although it's not a complicated trust such as an IRA trust or a revocable trust or an irrevocable trust designed to shelter assets from the costs of long-term care. The only asset you'll put in a Miller trust is a new trust checking account.

The sole purpose of the checking account in an irrevocable income trust is to receive your income every month and then pay most of that monthly income to the nursing home. At its core, it's nothing more than a funnel for your income. When you properly use an irrevocable income trust, no matter how high your income is, you bypass the income test. With proper advice and planning, no one should feel unable to qualify for Medicaid because of income.

This is not an instrument that will cause gifting penalties, and you need not set it up far in advance of need.

I'll talk more about gifting penalties and the five-year lookback applied by Medicaid when I address Medicaid asset limits, but you can set up a Miller trust at the time of need, right when nursing home or assisted living care becomes necessary, because a Miller trust has nothing to do with sheltering assets. It involves only your stream of monthly income. Once you set it up, you are required by law to send your income to an account in the name of the trust every month. The trust can pay for only certain things, primarily the nursing home or assisted living facility. But Medicaid allows other small expenditures from the Miller trust, such as health insurance and drug plan premiums. (Applicants who don't need a Miller trust can also pay insurance premiums from their income before they pay anything to the facility.)

Whether a Medicaid recipient uses a Miller trust or not, Medicaid rules allow recipients to keep a small amount of income for what's called a personal needs allowance. That varies from state to state as well, but in Arkansas it is only $40 a month.

Your income funnels into this Miller trust account. You keep your $40 allowance. You pay your health insurance premiums out of that Miller trust account, and then the trust funnels the rest to the nursing home. When using this procedure, it doesn't matter how high your income is—you still pass the income test. If you live in a state with an income limit, your income is higher than that limit, and you fail to use a Miller trust, or you don't use it correctly, you are going to be denied Medicaid because you failed the income test.

Though perhaps not identical in all states, the asset test is more uniform nationally than the income test. It is especially straightforward for a single person. A single applicant for Medicaid can own a house, a car, an irrevocable prepaid burial plan, and $2,000 worth of assets—and that's it. There is no mystery. There is no formula. It's $2,000. If you have cash value in life insurance exceeding $2,000 or a second vehicle, you could be flat broke without a penny in the bank but still be over the Medicaid asset limit.

Most people are over that limit. But before you try to solve that problem by transferring assets out of your name, you should know that Medicaid has a five-year lookback and some harsh transfer penalties. If you give anything away for less than fair market value within the five years leading up to the date of application for Medicaid benefits, Medicaid's going to assert a penalty period against you; during that period, you will not receive Medicaid assistance, even though you otherwise meet all rules for eligibility. That rule applies if you sell something for less than it was worth, but it also applies if you give an asset to your children without any compensation at all. Certain very limited exceptions apply to the transfer penalty rules, but in most situations, the following is what you have to prepare for: Medicaid will take the total value of whatever you transferred, subtract the compensation you received for that asset, if any, and divide the result by a figure called the penalty divisor. When you divide the value of the uncompensated transfer by the penalty divisor, the number you get is the number of months Medicaid will not help pay for the applicant's care in a long-term care facility.

In Arkansas right now, the penalty divisor is about $5,300. That number varies from state to state, but it is supposed to represent the average monthly cost of a nursing home in your state. Here's how it works: If you moved $53,000 during the five-year lookback in order to become qualified for Medicaid, your state will divide the $53,000 by the $5,300 penalty divisor. The result is that you are going to be approved for Medicaid but with a ten-month penalty period. In other words, you're going to have to wait ten months before you receive any type of Medicaid assistance in paying for long-term care because you moved money out of your name.

As I'll discuss in chapters 8 and 9, despite the five-year

lookback, it sometimes makes sense to move assets out of your name as you move toward nursing home care, even if doing so is going to result in a penalty period, because the math works out better for you. (See chapter 9 for some good examples of people who did that and why.) If you move assets, understand that you are not going to qualify for Medicaid right away unless those transfers occur at least five years before you apply for Medicaid assistance or those transfers fall into the extremely limited exceptions applicable in your state. That's how it works for a single person.

It's more complicated for a married couple. If one spouse needs a nursing home and the other spouse does not, the Medicaid rules are a little more generous for married people. Medicaid allows you to keep a house, one vehicle, and irrevocable prepaid burial plans, as is the case for a single applicant. But the amount of assets you can keep over and above these excluded assets varies from family to family, because what you can keep is based on a formula. The state is going to ask for all the couple's asset information as of the day the spouse in need of long-term care entered the nursing home. It's called the snapshot date. The state is going to take a snapshot of your financial position as of this key date. Within certain maximum and minimum limits, you will be allowed to keep one-half of whatever assets you had on that key date.

Take my grandparents' situation, for example. As I'm sure you recall, they had a $70,000 house and a rental house worth about the same amount. They also had $70,000 in financial assets. Had my grandfather been alive when my grandmother entered a nursing home, their main house would not have counted. That's their excluded asset. Their vehicle also would not have counted. The rental house and the $70,000 in financial assets would have counted. Their snapshot valuation would have been $140,000. That means they could have kept $70,000 worth of assets and still qualified for Medicaid.

In short, a married couple, unlike a single person, does not have to spend down to $2,000 to be eligible for Medicaid benefits. A couple has to spend down half of whatever they had when one spouse enters a facility. However, as I said, there are certain maximums and minimums, but they vary from state to state. The typical minimum is roughly $25,000. In other words, if you enter the facility and all you have is $30,000 in countable assets on your snapshot day, you don't have to spend half to get down to $15,000 for Medicaid coverage. You just have to spend down to your state minimum. If the minimum in your state is $25,000, you have to spend only $5,000 to reach the level at which you qualify for Medicaid coverage.

At the other end of the spectrum, if you had $500,000

when you entered the facility, you don't get to preserve half of it, or $250,000. The maximum in Arkansas and a lot of states is roughly $120,000. If you and your spouse had countable assets in excess of $240,000 when you entered the facility, your spouse is not going to get to keep half. Your spouse will be able to keep the state maximum, which in Arkansas would protect only $120,000.

You will need to talk to an attorney in your state to learn the minimums and maximums that apply to you, as well as to determine whether your state excludes other things from the list of countable assets. For example, some states will exclude the qualified retirement accounts owned by the spouse who is not entering a nursing home, but Arkansas does not. Finally, you will want to know if your state allows any transfers without penalty. For example, Arkansas and many other states allow parents to transfer assets to a child if that child is permanently disabled.

In addition to the asset protections given to spouses of nursing home residents, Medicaid includes some income protections for the spouse living at home. As I said earlier, the general rules say that you're going to send your income to the facility to cover as much of your care as possible, and then Medicaid pays the difference.

What happens when the spouse who brought in most of

the couple's income is entering a nursing home, and the spouse remaining at home receives only a small social security benefit in her own name, say, $800 a month? All the rest of the income was in the name of the higher-earning spouse—the one going to the nursing home.

The general rule would require the higher-earning spouse to turn over most of his income to the facility, and then Medicaid will pay the difference, but certain "spousal impoverishment rules" say that the spouse at home is going to get to keep a portion of her husband's income so that she will have a certain minimum income, a level set by the state. In Arkansas the state minimum is about $2,000 a month. If she has an income of only $800 in her own name, she will get to keep about $1,200 of her husband's income before the state determines what the nursing home resident owes for his care.

When both spouses need to enter a nursing home at the same time, these income and asset protections don't apply. In that case, the applicable rules for a couple are similar to those governing the eligibility of single applicants. This couple does not get to do a snapshot valuation, divide the assets in half, and save half of their assets up to the state maximum.

I need to address one final aspect of Medicaid, and it may

be the part that scares people the most. I said earlier that Medicaid recipients are permitted to keep their homes, and that's true. But if you still own that house when you die, the state gets to put a lien on it for the amount the state paid for your care during your lifetime. Your estate will technically own the house when you die, but the Medicaid lien will be similar to a mortgage on the property, and your heirs will wind up selling the house to reimburse the state.

This rule is often referred to as estate recovery. The rules governing a state's rights to a Medicaid recipient's estate vary from state to state, but they are definitely something to look out for. Taking into account the rules of estate recovery, and given that the Medicaid income rules do not allow a Medicaid recipient to retain any money to pay the usual expenses associated with home ownership—real estate taxes, insurance, utilities, and upkeep—most of my single Medicaid clients do not keep their house in their name when I do their planning for long-term care. For married applicants, the rules are often more lenient: Medicaid won't kick your spouse out of the house when you die, and if it winds up in the name of your widow or widower, estate recovery may never be an issue. But, again, this is an area that varies from state to state.

A lot of people say, "I don't want the nursing home to take my home." Nursing homes don't take homes. They don't want your house. Nursing homes just want you to pay their monthly bill. For that matter, Medicaid's not going to take your house. But unless your house is protected through early planning or, if you're lucky, through emergency planning permitted in your state, Medicaid is going to put a lien on it so that your heirs will be forced repay Medicaid for your care.

I have covered a lot of complicated information in this chapter. But if you take away just a few key points, I'll be happy. Long-term care is expensive, and the vast majority of seniors will need it. Of the four ways to pay for long-term care, the least desirable is from your own pocket, which was what my grandmother ended up doing. But now you have something she didn't have—the knowledge that other options exist.

One of those options, veterans' benefits, does not necessarily require planning long in advance of the need for assistance, but because of the informal lookback the VA already imposes and the formal lookback that has been proposed, preplanning is a good idea. On the other hand, long-term care insurance absolutely requires advance planning: if you wait until you need assistance to apply for coverage, you won't make it through underwriting. The third alternative, Medicaid, may be available to those who did not plan ahead but only if they were almost broke to start with. Families with assets cannot count on Medicaid benefits without some advance planning because of the five-year lookback and harsh gifting penalties.

In the next chapter, I explain in more detail what it means to plan in advance for veterans' benefits and Medicaid coverage and how to do it. But if after reading this chapter you are thinking, "It's already too late for my parents—they need long-term care now, and I can tell you without even reading the next chapter that they didn't do any planning at all," don't give up. Stick with me to chapter 9, where I'll show you some ways to pull a rabbit out of the hat. Even when families have failed to plan in advance for long-term care, it's often possible to put emergency plans into effect that preserve more assets than you ever thought possible.

CHAPTER EIGHT

Planning Ahead: The Safest Bet

A new client recently told me, "I want you to set up a trust that will protect my assets so that I won't go broke if I have to go to a nursing home. I don't want to spend everything I have on long-term care." She was younger than many of my clients who want to plan for long-term care, but she had been diagnosed with multiple sclerosis. She had gotten up early that morning to take extra medication so she would be able to keep her appointment with me.

She could see that she might need to move to a long-term care facility in the not-too-distant future, and she was trying to be realistic. She said, "I know that with my diagnosis and no spouse at home to help me stay there, a facility's probably in my future. But I am not loaded." She owned a house worth about $150,000, and she had about $100,000 altogether in various accounts. She said, "It may not be much to some people, but this is what I have. I want to do whatever I can to protect it." But as she explained what she wanted in more detail, we ran into problems. "I want a trust that will shelter my assets, so that if I need long-term care, I won't lose everything. But I want to be in complete control of my trust, and I want to be able to change it if I need to."

"Well, that's impossible," I told her. "I can't do that."

This is how I explained why it's impossible: "Picture a scale, like the scales of justice. One side represents your level of concern about sheltering your assets against long-term care costs. The other side represents your desire for flexibility and direct control of your trust. You have to weigh your priorities in order to decide how to set up your plan.

"If your bigger concern is sheltering assets against the cost of long-term care, and you're willing to give up some flexibility and direct control, then we can talk about asset protection. There is a trust that can do that. But if your biggest concern is flexibility and maintaining complete control, if that outweighs your concern about sheltering assets, then we need to talk basic estate planning. You'll probably want a more typical trust." Although she was young, she wasn't a candidate for long-term care insurance because of her serious diagnosis.

The choice confronting this client comes up time and again in my practice. It's not to say that you have to give everything away in order to plan for long-term care costs. That's not what I mean, and it's not what I usually recommend. But if you come in demanding absolute flexibility, so you can change your plan at any time, and you insist on complete control of your assets, we're not having a long-term care conversation, especially if you don't qualify for long-term care insurance.

Several of my clients have gotten bad diagnoses—Parkinson's, Alzheimer's, MS—and want to know what their options are before their disease becomes debilitating. Unlike someone who has had a bad stroke, at least these folks have time to plan.

The client with MS, who started out wanting complete control, decided during that first appointment that she needed to set up an irrevocable asset protection trust—a special trust designed specifically to shelter assets from long-term care costs. She named her daughter, a responsible person who was willing to manage the trust and quite capable of doing so, as her trustee. My client definitely wanted to be sure her daughter would inherit everything when she dies, so she told me, "If making my daughter trustee of this trust now is how I make sure that she gets everything when I'm gone, then I'm fine with it." Looking out for her daughter was important enough that she was willing to give up complete control of her trust.

She was lucky to have a responsible family member to appoint as trustee. Another client hired us to do an irrevocable asset protection trust, too, but he was in a rather different situation. He was far more concerned about protecting his estate against long-term care costs than he was about flexibility and control. He had two children and wanted everything to go to them. He couldn't imagine changing his mind, so what did flexibility matter? At first it seemed like this trust would be perfect for him too.

We had a couple of meetings to discuss his assets and how his plan would shelter those assets. He gathered up his financial information and other details I needed, and he came back for one last session before we started drafting his paperwork. Among the items we needed to discuss was who he wanted to name as trustee. The trustee, as you know by now, is the person who controls the day-to-day management of the trust. For the irrevocable asset protection trust to be valid, the trustee could not be my client, so we needed to name someone my client could count on. So I asked him, "Who do you want to name? You mentioned you have two boys. Should we name one or both of them?"

"I don't know," he told me. "I have had a lot of trouble deciding on that."

"Oh, okay," I replied. "Well, tell me—what are you thinking?"

"Well, you know, one of them, he lives in Montana, and I haven't seen him in a decade," the client said. "I don't actually know how to reach him. The other one, he's right here in Arkansas, but he's in prison, and I'm not 100 percent sure when he gets out. I don't know which one I should use."

True story. I don't know how that never came up in our previous meetings. I said, "Well, now that you mention it, I don't know that you're a great candidate for an irrevocable asset protection trust, unless—Do you have any other family we could involve?"

"Nope," he said. "That's it. My two boys are all I got."

My reaction was, "Well, maybe we need to look at something else, because we really can't name either one of them as trustee of your irrevocable trust."

Unlike the woman with MS, this man had no reasonable choice for trustee, which is essential for the type of plan he wanted. But an irrevocable trust probably wasn't a good option for him for another reason: he clearly had a dysfunctional family. The plan he was considering would have taken away his flexibility for dealing with the dysfunction down the road.

So what do I recommend to people who are worried about the high costs of long-term care and have some time to plan ahead? It didn't work out for this particular client, but the plan I most often use is the irrevocable asset protection trust. Recall that veterans' benefits and Medicaid both have asset limits, and Medicaid has a formal lookback on the transfer of assets. The VA imposes a frustrating informal lookback and may have a formal lookback soon. So any plan I propose must effectively decrease the countable assets held in the name of the person worried about long-term care so that, when he needs it, he can pass the asset test applicable to the benefit for which he wants to apply.

The irrevocable asset protection trust is one of the best means available for decreasing the countable assets of clients seeking to plan ahead for long-term care. The VA and Medicaid apply similar rules to asset protection trusts, so the trusts we use when planning to make someone eligible for either or both benefits are also similar. In fact, if you establish a trust that will satisfy VA rules, you've probably satisfied Medicaid rules, too, at least in most states, including Arkansas.

What distinguishes an asset protection trust from other types of trusts? First and foremost, only an irrevocable trust will shelter assets from the costs of long-term care, and that means you can't amend or revoke it. That does not mean the trustee cannot rearrange or even withdraw assets titled in the name of the trust. The irrevocable nature of this trust also does not mean a house titled in the name of the trust cannot be sold, nor does it mean the trustee cannot move money between accounts. It also does not mean you can't change banks or investment strategies or advisers, and it doesn't mean your trustee cannot use the trust funds to pay for certain expenses. All those things are permissible with this type of trust; the funds are not locked down. But the basic terms of the trust cannot be amended, and you cannot do away with the trust once it is established. That is why I explain to clients that they must balance their desire for flexibility against their desire to shelter their assets from the costs of long-term care when deciding whether to engage in this sort of planning.

The second distinguishing characteristic of an irrevocable asset protection trust is that the grantor who creates the trust cannot be the trustee of the trust. If you are the trustee of your own irrevocable trust, that means you're in control, and you cannot be in control if you want your trust to serve as a shelter for your assets. That is why my client with MS was lucky to have a responsible daughter to put in charge of her trust, and it's one reason why the client whose one son was in prison and the other estranged was not a good candidate for this type of planning. It's also the reason I explain to clients why they have to decide whether they are willing to give up control of their assets in order to shelter them. However, I need to add that while this rule about the trustee is a national one for veterans' benefits, and the State of Arkansas uses the same rule for Medicaid, some states do not have the same requirement in their Medicaid rules. Medicaid rules in some states allow the grantor of an irrevocable asset protection trust to also serve as trustee so long as the trust meets all other requirements. Be sure you work with an attorney in your state who knows what your options are.

It is important that you understand that not all estate-planning attorneys have knowledge and experience in the field of long-term care planning; many know little about qualifications for Medicaid and veterans' benefits. Attorneys who practice elder law, a field that specifically focuses on long-term care planning, are more likely to offer valuable guidance on how to plan for these benefit programs. When choosing an attorney, it is not sufficient to rely on advertising materials that vaguely refer to elder law. When researching your eligibility for veterans' benefits, you should work with an attorney who has been accredited by the VA. For all long-term care matters, you should consider working with a certified elder law attorney (CELA), a designation granted by the National Elder Law Foundation, an organization accredited by the American Bar Association. CELAs have demonstrated expertise in the field, passed a rigorous examination, and must meet the foundation's continuing education requirements to maintain that designation.

A third distinguishing characteristic of an asset protection trust is that the grantor who creates the trust cannot be a beneficiary of the trust. With a typical revocable trust, the grantor would be the lifetime beneficiary, and the grantor's children or other heirs would be death beneficiaries. But if you plan to use an irrevocable asset protection trust to shelter your assets from the costs of long-term care, you have to be comfortable with naming your children or other heirs as both the lifetime beneficiaries (with access to the trust assets while you're still living) and as the death beneficiaries (entitled to the inheritance at the time of your death). At no point can the grantor be a beneficiary of an irrevocable asset protection trust.

Using an irrevocable asset protection trust to shelter your assets from the costs of long-term care is better than transferring your assets directly to your children and hoping for the best. Although your children are beneficiaries of the irrevocable trust during your lifetime, your assets are not in your children's names. This distinction is important, as it protects those assets from your children's legal and financial troubles. Some clients think the best way to protect their assets from the costs of long-term care is to simply put those assets directly in their children's names. While that may very well shelter those assets from the parent's future long-term care costs, it subjects those assets to all of their children's legal risks, such as divorce and bankruptcy, as I mentioned in part 1. Direct transfers may also have adverse tax consequences, as I addressed in part 2. The irrevocable asset protection trust completely removes from your name and your control the assets you are seeking to protect, but it does not put those assets in your children's names or subject them to your children's legal risks.

Although an irrevocable asset protection trust cannot be amended or revoked, it may be possible to make some limited changes to this type of trust if your circumstances change. It is possible to build a little flexibility into these trusts but not nearly as much flexibility as you would have with a revocable trust.

First, a trustee who wants to resign can do so (or you may be able to force them to resign if you can provide sufficient motivation for them to do so). In some cases, you can even fire a trustee. If a trustee resigns or is fired, the successor trustee you named when you created the trust would take over. This isn't quite the same as retaining the authority to amend the trustee provisions, but it can help in certain situations.

I had a client who took advantage of this flexibility. Her husband had Parkinson's, and they did an irrevocable trust to shelter some assets so they could meet the VA asset test. They named their daughter, who lived nearby, as trustee. Then a son, who lived out of the country, was listed as the second trustee, just in case something happened to the daughter.

For reasons related to the trust, the daughter's relationship with her mother began to deteriorate badly. My client didn't regret doing the trust; she could see that it was extremely beneficial. Using the trust allowed her and her husband to meet the VA asset test, so the aid and attendance benefit contributed more than $2,100 a month toward their assisted living costs. But the trust apparently really hurt her relationship with her daughter.

When she came to see me, she said, "I want to change the

trust. I want our daughter out as trustee. I want our son to take over because I want to be able to get along with my daughter, and I just don't get along with her under this arrangement." I explained that she could not amend the trust because it was irrevocable, but if her daughter agreed to it, I might have a solution.

I called the daughter to state the obvious: "Your mother's not very happy with the setup."

She said, "Well, I'm not either. She won't listen to anything I say. I'm just trying to protect them."

So I told her, "There's actually an easy solution to this, if you're willing to do it. I can prepare a one-page resignation; you sign it and return it to me. And guess what? Your brother takes over as trustee. You don't have to do a thing with this trust or your parents' assets ever again." Arguably, under the terms of this particular trust, my client might have been able to fire her daughter as trustee, but because the trustee didn't commit any sort of fraud or wrongdoing (which would make the termination more clear-cut), that wasn't something we wanted to do.

"How's my brother going to do it?" the daughter wanted to know. "He's out of the country."

I said, "You let us worry about that. With e-mail and cell phones and faxes, it'll work, and it's what your mother really wants."

"Hey, you got it," the daughter told me. "Prepare it, and I'll sign it!"

As I hinted earlier, if a trustee commits fraud or otherwise mismanages a trust, I can't imagine a trust that wouldn't allow for termination of that trustee. But sometimes one person's mismanagement is another person's aggressive investment decision. If you have to go down the path of a forced termination, you'd better be prepared for a court battle.

Another way to build a little flexibility into an irrevocable trust is something called a power of appointment. When you create a trust, even an irrevocable trust, you can retain a power of appointment—it grants you the authority to modify the final disposition of trust assets through your last will and testament. In other words, if you know to ask for it, you can request that your estate-planning attorney include a retained power in your trust so that, if your circumstances change, you can later prepare a last will and testament that modifies the who-gets-what portion of your trust. Let's say you have an irrevocable trust that named your three children as equal beneficiaries, but then you have a falling out with one of them. Or maybe you ended up using half your estate to get one child out of legal trouble. You might want to amend your trust so that child no longer receives an equal third of your trust when you die. But you can't amend your trust; it's irrevocable. You can, on the other hand, execute a formal last will and testament to expressly exercise the power of appointment you retained, and by doing so, you can modify the percentage of assets that child will receive through your trust.

You might be thinking, "That sure sounds like a trust amendment to me." You're right. It does, and it's just one more demonstration that these trusts can allow a little more flexibility than people realize.

But you need to tell your lawyer that you want to retain a power of appointment in your trust. I have reviewed many irrevocable trusts prepared by other lawyers that did not include a retained power of appointment. I have also reviewed trusts that contain a power of appointment but one that allows the grantor only to add charitable beneficiaries to the trust through a last will and testament, not necessarily the power to adjust the shares of the beneficiaries named in the document. An *unrestricted power of appointment* isn't a term you'd expect to find in a standard irrevocable trust. I doubt you'd find it in any trust form you could pull from the Internet. This is one reason to avoid online or prepackaged estate-planning vehicles, because they are not going to have that kind of flexibility built in, nor would you know how to use those terms if they were there. It's not only a matter of deciding whether you want a revocable or irrevocable trust. There is much more to it than people realize.

Online trust forms and inexperienced attorneys are likely to miss another big issue. It involves the interaction of the second and third strands of planning. Most irrevocable trusts are written so that beneficiaries do not receive a stepped-up capital gains tax basis when the grantor dies. This provision can be extremely important if the trust owns a house with a low basis or stocks that were purchased years ago for a fraction of their current value.

Lawyers writing irrevocable trusts do not forget to include or deliberately omit terms designed to give the beneficiaries favorable capital gains tax treatment. On the contrary, smart estate-planning attorneys intentionally add special terms to an irrevocable trust to get the tax benefits that are automatic with a revocable trust. Out of concern for their clients, accountants and financial advisers have insisted to me that using an irrevocable trust automatically means loss of the stepped-up tax basis. While it is true that the standard wording in an irrevocable trust would result in the outcome they fear, careful drafting can avoid the problem. They didn't realize that because they hardly ever see terms like that.

I'll make the point again—not all trusts are created equal. A general practice attorney might charge $1,000 to draw up a trust, perhaps even less. You also could pull free or low-cost trust forms off the Internet. But you get what you pay for. And when it comes to irrevocable asset protection trusts, an awful lot can go wrong if you don't do it right.

Think of an irrevocable trust as a safe. You give the combination to whomever you name as trustee, but you do not give the combination to the government or the nursing home—or, for that matter, to yourself. You have locked your assets in a safe, but you have not given them away. You have given control—the combination to the safe—to someone else, someone you trust to serve as your trustee. Yes, you give up flexibility and control, but you don't put your assets at risk like you would with direct gifts to your children, and you shelter those assets from the high costs of long-term care.

How do you decide what to put in an irrevocable asset protection trust? Good question. You have to consider what type of long-term care benefits you are most likely to file for and the asset restrictions you will face. What goes into the trust varies from grantor to grantor—it's a personal decision. But I can give you some general guidelines.

An asset that almost never goes into an asset protection trust is the regular checking account—the one you use to receive your income deposits and pay your bills. I don't intend to interfere with your day-to-day activities when setting up a trust like this, and changing your regular checking account would likely interrupt your income deposits because you'd have to get a new account number and reroute the deposits. Now, if you regularly keep a very high balance in your regular checking account, you might consider reducing that balance so that more assets are sheltered in your trust and fewer sit in your checking account. What's a high balance? That's up to you. But Medicaid, for example, has a five-year lookback, so you don't have to reduce your assets to $2,000 today; you're not going to file for Medicaid for at least five years. It's fine if you have a little bit of a cushion in your checking account. Under current law, veterans' benefits do not have a lookback, so you could set up a trust like this the month before you file for benefits. But even a single person applying for veterans' benefits can have as much as $40,000, so you don't have to reduce your checking account to an uncomfortable level.

Even if someone has a little too much money in his or her

name and not in trust near the end of the Medicaid five-year lookback, I assure you that person will inevitably have some expenses while preparing for the move to a nursing home. It will be easy to spend down a modest amount. You just don't want to leave a large sum unprotected.

Another asset we almost never put into an asset protection trust is an IRA or other retirement account. We wouldn't retitle those accounts in the name of any type of trust—you can't, really. You can name an IRA trust as *beneficiary* of a retirement account, but no trust can own a retirement account. The only thing you could do is cash out the account, pay the taxes, and put whatever's left into the trust. My clients are usually not interested in creating a large immediate tax liability, even when they want to plan ahead for long-term care expenses. Clients who have large IRAs and want to plan ahead for Medicaid coverage will either choose not to use an asset protection trust or they'll use one, but they will leave their regular checking account and their IRAs out of the trust and live off those IRAs during the five-year lookback. They'll be reducing them gradually over time instead of cashing them out all at once. Use of an asset protection trust might still make sense if they have substantial nonretirement assets to protect.

The first asset we almost always include in the asset protection trust is the house. Whether the client plans to sell or keep it, and whether their emphasis is Medicaid or veterans' benefits, the wise client puts the house in the trust. Neither Medicaid nor the VA includes the house as a countable asset, so putting the house in the asset protection trust is not essential to meet either asset test. But with Medicaid, you have to watch out for estate recovery. Putting the house in an asset protection trust shields it from liens the state would otherwise try to place on it. Selling the house would likely make the homeowner ineligible for either benefit, unless the asset protection trust sheltered the house and the trustee sold it. And, of course, don't forget about the first strand of planning. The asset protection trust will make sure the house gets where you want it to go without probate court.

Beyond those three assets, it's hard to set out a general rule about what goes into an asset protection trust and what does not. You just have to think about that scale again. Anything you title in the name of the asset protection trust will be sheltered. Anything you leave out will remain in your direct control, but you may be forced to use an asset that remains outside the trust to pay for long-term care or, in the case of your home, the state may put a lien against it when you die. If your desire to protect an asset is greater than your desire to maintain control of it, you'll put it in the trust. It's as simple as that.

When funding the asset protection trust, you have to keep in mind why you created it. For example, if a single person is trying to become immediately eligible for veterans' benefits by using an asset protection trust, which is possible under current rules since there is no lookback, she must fund the trust with all of her assets in excess of the $40,000 asset limit. But a client trying to prepare in advance for Medicaid would have more flexibility in his funding. There's no magic number he's shooting for right now. He simply needs to shelter everything he can, everything that can be titled in the name of the trust without adverse consequences, like an immediate tax hit for cashing in an IRA. But he should leave out of the trust whatever level of assets he feels he needs to be comfortable during the five-year lookback.

Again, I rarely recommend moving IRAs because of the immediate tax consequences. But sometimes there's a decision to be made with IRAs. If a couple seeking to immediately qualify for veterans' benefits has a $100,000 IRA, they will have to do something with at least a portion of those funds if they expect to meet the VA asset test. On the other hand, if that same couple is not trying to immediately qualify for veterans' benefits but instead is simply trying to plan ahead for Medicaid, they might decide to fund their trust with everything except their checking account and their IRA. Then they might draw a little more heavily from the IRA to meet expenses during the next five years since it is their only substantial unprotected asset.

The bottom line, of course, is that you need to shelter your assets in advance. You don't want to wait until you need long-term care to shelter those assets. For Medicaid, the lookback period is clear-cut: five years. Veterans' benefits have no formal lookback under current law, but the informal lookback is frustrating enough to warrant planning as far ahead as you can. And the proposed three-year lookback will make planning ahead even more essential.

When planning ahead for long-term care benefits, it is essential that you understand what type of estate plan you have. I can't tell you how often—probably once a month—someone comes into my office and says, "Okay, Dad needs a nursing home now. Thank goodness we have a trust, so none of their assets are in their name. We're good, right?" Wrong. In many cases when I review their documents, I find that all they have is a basic revocable trust. Everything in that trust counts. People get really frustrated. "Well, why did my lawyer tell me everything was protected?"

I say, "Protected from what?" Everything in a revocable trust is protected from probate court, if that's what they meant, but nothing in their revocable trust is protected from long-term care expenses.

Another thing everyone needs to recognize is that trying to plan on their own can cause a bigger mess than doing nothing at all. Consider the situation of spouses who know that one of them is going to need a nursing home soon. They'll need Medicaid to help pay for it. One spouse is relatively healthy, but the other is not. Medicaid rules say their house doesn't count against them, and we can transfer their house without penalty to the spouse who will continue to live there. We can do it without making the house vulnerable to Medicaid liens that would apply if the infirm spouse had owned the house and died after receiving Medicaid coverage.

But too many people rush out and deed their home to their children without legal advice. Because we know the Medicaid rules on estate recovery, we could have protected that house without creating any Medicaid penalties. Instead, the decision to deed it to the kids creates a totally unnecessary Medicaid penalty, and they've also handed their kids an unfavorable tax basis for the house.

What is important to understand about Medicaid is that it has two different rules that relate to the transfer of assets. The first rule is the five-year lookback, which I've addressed throughout this chapter. The second one is the actual gifting *penalty*. The five-year lookback is simply a window through which Medicaid is allowed to look at what you've done with your assets. The gifting penalty applies to any transfer of assets that occurred during that period. If you moved an asset six months ago, it doesn't necessarily mean that you're not going to get any Medicaid coverage for five years. The penalty will be based on the value of the asset you transferred.

Let's say a woman deeded her small house, worth about $75,000, to her son six months before she entered a nursing home. That has negative tax consequences, but maybe she didn't know or care about that. She didn't expect to need a nursing home after only six months; she thought she might be able to stay at home for the next five years, but she grossly miscalculated. Medicaid is not going to deny her coverage for five years just because she gave her son a $75,000 house six months ago. Medicaid is going to take the total value of the asset she transferred and divide it by the penalty divisor. In Arkansas, the current penalty divisor of about $5,300 would result in a penalty period of approximately fourteen months. It'll be hard to figure out how to pay the nursing home during this waiting period, but fourteen months is a lot shorter than the four and a half years she might have expected if she had even vague knowledge of the five-year lookback.

But say you moved a lot of assets four years ago, and now you need nursing home care. Your best plan might be simply to wait one more year before filing for benefits. You might have to go to the nursing home and pay for it out of pocket until the five-year lookback runs out on the transfers you made. But if you can afford it, there's no reason you can't move to a nursing home after transferring significant assets four years ago. You simply wait to apply for Medicaid coverage until five years have passed since you made those transfers.

Be careful with this. The scenario I just described is different from the one involving the woman who transferred a small asset six months ago and intentionally filed for Medicaid during the five-year lookback to start the clock on a short gifting penalty. If you go ahead and file for Medicaid in the fourth year after a *large* transfer, you will be assigned a gifting penalty that will extend far beyond the five-year lookback you were shooting for. And that's exactly what it'll do—extend beyond the five-year anniversary of the transfer you made. Gifting penalties can extend beyond the five-year lookback. Medicaid can't penalize you for transfers that occurred *more than five years* before the date of application for benefits. If you transferred substantial assets within five years of needing nursing home care, you don't want to apply for Medicaid benefits to pay for your care until the lookback period runs out.

In my opinion, only the irrevocable asset protection trust

addresses all three strands of planning. It will ensure that your assets go where you want them to go without the necessity of probate (the first strand), it will give your beneficiaries a stepped-up capital gains tax basis if drafted properly (the second strand), and it will shelter your assets against the high costs of long-term care (the third strand).

But remember: Not all irrevocable trusts are created equal. An improperly drafted irrevocable trust—arguably, the typical irrevocable trust—can create horrible tax consequences. Think about my client whose mother inherited the forty-acre parcel that was nearly worthless when she became the owner. When her daughter came to me, it was worth more than $1 million.

If her mother threw that land into a typical irrevocable trust, one that did not include terms to ensure the daughter received the property with a stepped-up tax basis upon the mother's death, the mother might have immediately made herself eligible for veterans' benefits or been ready for Medicaid assistance after the five-year lookback, but she would end up losing much more money in capital gains taxes when her daughter eventually sold the property for a huge taxable profit.

When you want to plan ahead for long-term care benefits, which is your safest option, you've got to pull out that scale and weigh your desire for control and flexibility against your desire to protect your assets. That will guide you in making your decision. But for those who have failed to plan ahead, an irrevocable asset protection trust might still help with an immediate application for veterans' benefits, if the VA has not imposed a lookback by the time you read this book. In the next chapter, I discuss some emergency techniques that are available to people who have done no planning, suddenly face the immediate need to enter a nursing home, and want or need Medicaid to pay for it.

CHAPTER NINE

Pulling a Rabbit from the Hat: Creative Solutions for Those Who Didn't Plan Ahead

Although planning ahead for long-term care benefits is by far the safest option, some people don't do it. That's a characteristic of being human, especially if planning ahead means making hard choices and tackling things we'd rather not think about, or if planning ahead simply is difficult because of a tough family situation or a particularly complex mix of assets.

A lot of people figure that since they didn't plan ahead, they will just have to pay for their nursing home care out of pocket until all their money is gone. That's not necessarily the case and, in fact, is almost never the best option.

Let's say that you are over the asset limit for Medicaid eligibility, but you are not over the limit by $500,000. You are over the limit by only a modest amount—say $100,000. As I discussed in chapter 8, if you transferred assets out of your name within the last five years, you have not necessarily created a period of ineligibility for the next five years. By transferring assets out of your name and then filing for Medicaid, if you handle the process right, you'll actually get a Medicaid approval, but that approval will come with a penalty period—which might be more appropriately thought of as a waiting period.

When we use the term *penalty period*, some people think they've done something wrong or illegal, like a penalty in sports or a penalty in taxes. It's not that kind of penalty—it's really a period during which you have to wait for Medicaid coverage. In fact, when you understand the Medicaid gifting rules, you may intentionally create a waiting period because you crunched the numbers and found it would be more advantageous to transfer those assets than it would be to hold on to them and continue paying privately for nursing home care indefinitely.

My grandmother's story provides an illustration of what I'm talking about. You'll recall that her home, worth about $70,000, was in her name. She also had a $70,000 rental house. Then she had about $70,000 in financial accounts. That's $210,000 in total assets that we would have needed to get out of her name to make her eligible for assistance in paying for her nursing home care. You would be right in assuming that an outright transfer of all my grandmother's assets would have resulted in a penalty period of more than thirty-nine months using Arkansas's penalty divisor ($210,000 ÷ $5,300). Nearly three and a half years is a long time, but it's better than simply paying out of pocket until she runs out of money, and it's better than transferring those assets and waiting out the five-year lookback. But we could have done better than that in her case.

A lot of people might assume that the first thing she should have done was get the properties out of her name by deeding them to her kids. Since I'm describing an emergency Medicaid planning situation, the tax lessons from part 2 might have to take a backseat to Medicaid planning, so deeding the property to the kids is certainly an option. However, she should not use regular quitclaim deeds. Here's what I would have told my grandmother to do, if I had known then what I know now.

First, I would have said, "Let's not deed away 100 percent

of your interest in your rental house. Let's create a joint tenancy between you and your daughter. You deed her a one-half interest in the rental property, and we will set up the deed so that you are joint tenants with right of survivorship." (See chapter 2.) Setting the deed up this way means her daughter will own 100 percent of the house after my grandmother's death, but it also means that, under Medicaid law in Arkansas, it's no longer a countable asset. Property owned by two people under a joint tenancy with right of survivorship—in this case, mother and daughter—is not a countable asset if the daughter signs a form saying she refuses to sell the property.

Under this arrangement, we have transferred the rental house so it does not count against my grandmother for Medicaid purposes, and it will not pass through probate at my grandmother's death. And doing it this way does not cost her $70,000 worth of gifting penalty. It costs her half that, $35,000, because my grandmother retains a one-half interest. Her interest does not count against her $2,000 asset limit because of the joint ownership rule, but the method of transfer results in half the penalty that an outright transfer would incur.

My grandmother also owned the house she had been living in. Although the house does not count against her for purposes of the asset test, out of concern for Medicaid liens at death, we could do the same thing with her residence that we did with the rental house. We could do a joint tenancy deed with that house, giving my dad a one-half interest. Better yet, my grandmother could do a life estate deed, where she deeds a remainder interest in the house to my dad, but she retains the right to live in and use the house as long as she sees fit (see chapter 2). Here's the interesting thing: if she retains a life estate in the house, my dad gets a stepped-up capital gains tax basis for that property at her death. Using a life estate deed in a situation like this can address all three strands of planning: she gets the property out of her name and into my dad's name to protect it from the possibility of Medicaid liens, my dad receives advantageous tax treatment at her death, and my dad inherits the property without probate. Be forewarned, however, that some states do allow estate recovery against a house in a situation like this, so talk with a knowledgeable attorney in your state so you know what your options are. Remember, my grandmother didn't have to deed her house to meet the Medicaid asset test, since it was an excluded asset. But we would have done it to keep the house out of probate and to avoid Medicaid liens at the time of death.

This sort of deed results in a penalty period, just like the quitclaim deed we didn't use or the joint tenancy deed we used with the rental house, but Medicaid says that the right my grandmother retained—the right to live in and use that property—carries with it a retained monetary value that reduces the penalty on what my grandmother transferred to my dad. According to the actuarial charts that Medicaid uses, that monetary value—that life estate—could be worth as much as half of the value of the property for a person in her seventies. She doesn't get hit with a penalty period for transferring a $70,000 asset. The penalty period is based only on the value of the house after it is reduced by the value of the retained life estate, which is only $35,000 in this example.

So now we have transferred real estate worth $140,000, but because of the way we executed the transfers, my grandmother's penalty period is going to be based on the transfer of only $70,000 worth of real estate, half the value of each property.

We still have the $70,000 in financial assets to consider. We could simply transfer all of it to her children, but before we do that, I would check to see if she has prepaid her burial expenses. If not, it's time to do that (remember: a prepaid burial plan is not a countable asset), so right now, while she has the money to do it, she'll pay 100 percent of whatever her funeral will cost.

You could easily spend $10,000 in legal fees to set all this up, but that too will come out of her remaining financial assets. That helps spend down the assets so that she is that much closer to Medicaid coverage without additional gifting penalties. Remember, spending money on my grandmother's needs does not cause a gifting penalty; only gifts or transfers factor into the penalty calculation. Let's say my grandmother spent $10,000 to prepay her funeral and $10,000 to a lawyer for Medicaid planning. (I was still in college when she should have been doing this sort of planning, so I couldn't have done it for her.) Now her financial assets have been reduced from $70,000 to $50,000.

We already know that my grandmother won't be covered by Medicaid immediately, so I'd suggest she pay the upcoming month's nursing home bill. It costs $5,000 a month, so she has reduced her bank account balance to $45,000. She gives that $45,000 to her other son, my uncle.

Instead of having gifted assets valued at $210,000 and facing a waiting period of more than thirty-nine months, my grandmother has gifted $70,000 in real estate—half the value of each house because of the way we prepared the deeds—and $45,000 in cash, a total of $115,000. That would result in a waiting period of less than twenty-two months ($115,000 ÷ $5,300). But she can save still more money.

When she files for Medicaid, everything has been intentionally removed from her name, so Medicaid is not going to deny her application. She meets the asset test. She will receive an approval with a penalty period because of the asset transfers, so Medicaid will not start helping with her nursing home bill right away.

So how will she pay for her care during those twenty-two months? She gets only $2,500 a month between my grandfather's pension and her social security. But her nursing home costs $5,000 a month. What's the family going to do? My uncle is going to dip into that $45,000 that my grandmother gave him to pay the difference.

Here's the interesting thing: Medicaid has a rule that says if you return any portion of the gifted funds, whether you do it in a lump sum or over time, whether you do it before you file for Medicaid or after you apply, Medicaid has to adjust the penalty period accordingly. I need to warn you again that this is another rule that can vary from state to state, so be sure you know how your state treats the return of gifted assets before engaging in this sort of planning. After fifteen months, my uncle has contributed $37,500 toward my grandmother's nursing home bill from the cash my grandmother transferred to him—he pays the $2,500 shortfall her income doesn't cover in each of the fifteen months for total contributions of $37,500. If the family goes back to Medicaid with proof of the payments he made over and above what her income would cover, in Arkansas, Medicaid will recalculate the penalty period using a total gift amount of $77,500 instead of the $115,000 it originally used ($115,000 - $37,500). That means my grandmother's new penalty period is just under fifteen months ($77,500 ÷ $5,300). By doing what my uncle was going to have to do anyway—use the money my grandmother gave him to help cover the cost of her nursing home during her waiting period—he reduced my grandmother's waiting period by about seven months (from the original twenty-two months to fifteen months).

The end result of this plan is that my grandmother's rental property and her house are safely in the hands of her children, about $7,500 of her cash still remains in my uncle's name, her burial and legal fees are covered, and my grandmother is now fully covered by Medicaid after a waiting period of only fifteen months. She saved $147,500 worth of assets ($70,000 rental house, $70,000 house, and $7,500 in cash) while still qualifying for Medicaid in a comparatively short period of time.

My grandmother could have had a waiting period of more than thirty-nine months if she had not handled her transfers in the optimal way. Instead, her penalty started out at less than two years. But after only fifteen months, because of the adjustment in the penalty along the way, my grandmother is fully covered by Medicaid. That's just one example of pulling a rabbit out of a hat.

In this same example, after my grandmother makes her transfers, applies for Medicaid, and receives a twenty-two-month penalty period, what prevents her from filing for VA benefits? Nothing. She doesn't have any money in her name and therefore would meet the VA asset test under any analysis, and the VA has no lookback. She's spending all her monthly income on the nursing home bill, so she meets the VA's income test. She could have filed for veterans' benefits when she filed for Medicaid. Instead, of the $2,500 in monthly income she had to contribute toward the cost of her care each month, she would have had $3,650, because she would have qualified for about $1,150 a month in aid and assistance. My uncle would have had to contribute only $1,350 each month toward her care from the gifted money, saving even more of the funds she had transferred to him. The higher your income, the less money your children have to contribute to the cost of care and the more they end up saving.

If my grandmother had received the aid and attendance benefit, my uncle would have contributed to my grandmother's nursing home costs for seventeen months instead of fifteen, but the overall contributions would have totaled only $23,000 instead of $37,500 without the aid and attendance benefit. Each month for seventeen months, my uncle would use $1,350 of the funds my grandmother transferred to him to make up the shortfall at the nursing home. After contributing for seventeen months, he has returned $23,000 of the gifted funds ($1,350 × 17 months). Medicaid then recalculates the penalty period using a total gift amount of $92,000 instead of $115,000 ($115,000 - $23,000), resulting in a final penalty period of seventeen months. Now, almost half of the originally gifted funds remain—about $22,000—and my grandmother is fully covered by Medicaid. In some cases Medicaid and veterans' benefits can go hand in hand.

Taking this example one step further, since the VA does not yet have a lookback, she could have transferred her assets even sooner and filed for veterans' benefits as soon as she moved to an assisted living facility (before her move to the nursing home). Then her income of $2,500 a month, plus $1,150 in VA benefits, would have allowed her to cover the cost of her stay in assisted living without dipping into her savings, and perhaps the Medicaid five-year lookback would have run out before she even moved to a nursing home. In that case, she would have received Medicaid coverage almost immediately after entering the nursing home instead of waiting out a penalty period. Medicaid cannot penalize someone for transfers that occurred more than five years before application for benefits. In my grandmother's case, we know she lived in assisted living for only about a year, so things wouldn't have worked out that way. But trying to plan for the five-year lookback would have cost her nothing extra—the same penalty calculations apply whether you gift assets one year or one month before moving to a nursing home and applying for Medicaid.

And what if she had stayed in assisted living for four and a half years and then had the stroke that sent her to a nursing home? That's one of those situations where my best advice is to be patient: Pay for the nursing home care out of pocket for the next six months using her income and the gifted funds and then file for Medicaid after the five-year lookback has expired. If she files for Medicaid immediately upon entering the nursing home, even if her transfer of assets occurred four and a half years earlier, Medicaid would still assess a twenty-two-month penalty period.

This example contains several key lessons. Even though you think you're going to need Medicaid to pay for your nursing home care, and you know that Medicaid might put a lien on your house when you die, don't rush out and deed your house outright to your kids. There's probably going to be a better way to handle that. And don't assume that you are going to have to pay for your care out of pocket for five years, because that's not necessarily the case if you really understand the gifting rules. Finally, don't overlook veterans' benefits, even if qualifying for Medicaid is your primary goal.

You'll recall that Medicaid rules for married couples are quite different from the rules that apply to single applicants. Consider the example of a couple in their eighties; the husband has always been independent and quite private, but now that his wife needs nursing home care, he consults my firm to find out how he can save some of the money he worked so hard all his life to accumulate. He has always paid his own way and taken care of his own affairs. He didn't want or need anybody's help, and he never consulted a lawyer before for any reason, so I know this is hard for him.

"I don't know what I'm going to do," he tells me. "My wife is over at the nursing home now for rehabilitation. I had always planned to bring her home when the rehab ended, but I'm being more realistic now, and I realize that's not going to happen. The nursing home wasn't rude or anything, but they said, considering her lack of progress, they just don't see her ever being able to go home.

"They told me when her rehab ends, which is probably

going to be two weeks from today, they're going to start sending me a bill for $6,000 a month. I don't know what to do. I mean, I make $3,000 a month myself, but she brings in only about $1,000 in social security, so combined we have only $4,000 a month. I can't even pay the nursing home bill out of our income, much less meet my own expenses. I still have a house, utilities, bills. I don't know what to do."

Let's say his house is worth $200,000 and that he has about $200,000 in other financial resources. "I mean, I've got some money here," he tells me, "but I've already calculated $6,000 a month is going to be $72,000 a year out of our pocket. If she stays there a couple of years, I'll go broke."

I say, "Well, not exactly. You've got your income coming in to help, but, yes, I see what you're saying—this is bad."

"Well, I need to do whatever I can do," he says. "I want to get some help."

We are able to show him a way to get Medicaid by using something called a Medicaid-qualified annuity, and his wife can qualify for Medicaid without their spending down in the traditional way or wasting money. First, we need to protect his house. Under Arkansas rules, all we have to do is get her name off the deed, transferring it into his name only. Why? Because if he happens to die first, it would go back to her as co-owner if her name remains on the deed. As a widow, she'd be a single person on Medicaid with a home. She'd face Medicaid liens.

We don't gift the home to the children, since that would cause gifting penalties. We simply take her name off the deed and then work with him on a plan to avoid probate without sending assets back her way if he dies first. A beneficiary deed (see chapter 2) might be the answer because it also protects the house from probate—we can't forget about the first strand of planning. And the recipient of a beneficiary deed receives the step up in tax basis everybody wants, so we will have addressed the second strand as well.

He would still have the $200,000 to deal with. Remember, he's allowed to keep half of whatever they had as a couple when she enters the nursing home. So the rules protected $100,000 right off the top. Somehow we need to get her name off that money and into his name alone, whether he keeps it in a checking or savings account, a CD, money market investment, stocks, bonds—it doesn't matter. He can have $100,000 worth of assets in his name. The other $100,000 is assigned to her. There's no reason to try to get her name off that money right now, because Medicaid doesn't care if it's in his name or her name. Medicaid says anything in either name counts the same and puts her over the limit.

Here's what we can do. Any spending that he needs to do can come out of her half, so long as the money is spent to benefit either spouse. So if he decides to hire me to do the work, her half of the assets can pay the legal fees, say, $10,000. If he has planned any home repairs such as a new roof, or if his truck needs new tires, those expenses can come out of her side too. If one or both spouses need a prepaid burial plan, we can take care of those expenses for both spouses out of her half. In this case, without wasting any money, my client can easily spend $30,000 or more on legitimate needs before moving to the next step of the plan.

The next step involves the Medicaid-qualified annuity. Assets owned by either spouse count against the wife in this situation, but his income does not count against her when she applies for Medicaid. Her income is the only income Medicaid takes into account when determining her eligibility under the income test. We take that remaining $70,000 or so and pour it into an annuity with special terms designed to satisfy Medicaid rules, and that annuity pays protected monthly income to him. It's a single-premium immediate annuity, which means you pay a single one-time premium. You don't pay into this over time. You give the annuity company $70,000, and in exchange it gives you a contract. It's an irrevocable purchase, so you can never get the $70,000 back in a lump sum, but the contract guarantees you a set monthly income stream, which is protected because it's payable only to the spouse living at home.

That contract says the annuity company promises to pay Mr. Smith $1,200 per month for the next five years ($72,000 in all), in exchange for his $70,000 premium. Neither the Federal Deposit Insurance Corporation nor any other government entity insures the money, but the company that issues the contract guarantees it. It is not tied to the stock market. It pays him a guaranteed $1,200 a month backed by the strength of the financial institution that issues the contract.

Once he signs the contract and hands over the $70,000, his wife is immediately qualified for Medicaid. When I say that, most people's jaws drop. They say, "That sounds too good to be true. This can't work." It absolutely does. I don't know if Congress meant to do it, or if it is an unintended loophole, but if you meet all the rules for Medicaid-qualified annuities, this purchase results in protected income for the spouse living at home and immediate qualification for Medicaid for the spouse in the facility.

She still has to send her $1,000 a month to the nursing home every month, but the cost of her care is $6,000 a month. Medicaid covers the rest. Really, she's not even going to pay the full $1,000, because she can keep $40 a month for her personal needs allowance, and she keeps enough to cover her own health insurance and drug plan premiums.

Meanwhile, he still has his home, $100,000 in his name alone, all his own income, plus a new $1,200 monthly income stream generated by the annuity. And they have already prepaid their legal fees and burial costs and are set to avoid probate.

That is the way we would handle the case of a married couple facing a huge nursing home bill for one spouse when the other spouse is healthy and living at home. Here's another twist. Let's say a year down the road their daughter calls and tells me, "Justin, I think we messed up."

"Why? What happened?"

"Dad needs a nursing home now. We just put everything in his name, and he needs a nursing home. How's he going to get Medicaid?"

He probably won't get Medicaid under these circumstances, but we don't need it for him because he's a veteran. He could be entitled to veterans' benefits. If he goes to a nursing home, and his income is not enough to cover his nursing home bill, we can file for veterans' benefits for him. As a married veteran, he'd get about $2,100 a month on top of his current income and his annuity payment. He's got $3,000 coming in from his own income sources each month, plus the $1,200 from the annuity we created. Another $2,100 from the VA, and he has the $6,000 he needs to pay his nursing home bill plus $300 to pay his health insurance premiums. If he still has $100,000 in assets in his name, he might have to do a little maneuvering to meet the VA asset test. But he still doesn't have to worry about the house since the VA does not put liens on houses the way Medicaid does.

The result of our planning is that Medicaid is paying for the wife's nursing home, and he has an annuity income that we originally thought he wouldn't need—he'd just stash the money in a savings account. It turns out that he does need it, because he needs a nursing home himself.

The Medicaid-qualified annuity is not the only way to spend down for Medicaid qualification when one spouse remains at home. Plenty of couples tell me that the house they want to pass down to their kids needs new carpeting, its kitchen has not been updated since the 1960s, the roof needs to be replaced, and the driveway is full of potholes.

Those repairs and updates could cost $30,000 or more. The better condition the house is in when the kids inherit it, the more money they're going to get when they sell it, so this could be a pretty good investment.

What about the car? They probably own a 1998 sedan that's no longer dependable. So instead of just replacing the tires, let's trade her sedan in for a new, fuel-efficient, low-maintenance car. And guess what? They can pass that car on to the kids. In many circumstances, it is possible to spend down in an efficient and prudent manner without using a Medicaid-qualified annuity.

That's two approaches for the same couple who had not planned for their long-term care expenses. Despite the lack of advance planning, we still pulled a rabbit out of the hat and got one spouse qualified for Medicaid and the other for a VA benefit.

In a few cases, we can do yet another transfer of an asset without incurring a penalty. Just as there's no penalty for transferring a house between spouses, there's no penalty for transferring assets to a disabled child. I have had clients come to me because they need nursing home care and had done no advance planning to pay for it. But what they really were worried about was the disabled adult child they've been caring for.

Arkansas and most other states have exceptions that allow you to transfer assets to a disabled child, either outright or through a special needs trust, without any Medicaid penalty at all. If you use a trust to make those transfers, you can include not only special needs trust provisions to protect the child's eligibility for benefits but also provisions to ensure the child receives a stepped-up tax basis on property you pass through the trust. This can work even if the adult child is not necessarily dependent on his parents as a result of his disability. The exception applies so long as the government has determined the child is disabled.

Many states have another exception you should be aware of: the caregiver child exception. Note that it's a caregiver *child* exception, not a caregiver *grandchild* or a caregiver *friend* or a caregiver *niece* exception—it works only for children. If a child has been living in your home with you as a full-time caregiver for at least two years, because that's the only way you can stay at home, and your doctor certifies that you needed help to stay home, you can transfer your house—not all your assets, only your house—to that caregiver child without penalty, even if that child owns another house. It's kind of a reward, an encouragement, that says, "If you'll move in with Mom or Dad to help them stay at home longer so the Medicaid program doesn't have to pay the nursing home for as long, they can transfer their house to you to thank you for that care."

Those are two other exceptions in the law that we can use to pull a rabbit out of the hat in an emergency situation. However, the point of this chapter is not to tell you about every trick a good elder law attorney might know. I just wanted to give you some idea of the possibilities—and let you know that possibilities do exist. That's why you need advice from good, competent professionals who know the laws of your state.

Having said that, I don't want you to think you can avoid planning ahead and just wing it if you need nursing home care. Yes, sometimes we can pull rabbits out of a hat, but planning ahead is always the safest option, and it almost always results in more assets saved than emergency planning can save.

I've had several clients proudly tell me, "I've helped Mom as best I can. We've done everything. We've gotten her assets taken care of; we're right down to the end. Basically, we're about out of money, and I guess I need your help to get her on Medicaid now."

What? Why didn't you call me two years ago, before you were out of money? I don't say that, of course. Instead, I say, "Okay, we'll play the hand we've been dealt. What can we do now to make this as efficient as possible?" And we take it from there. But at that point, a lot of our options are closed, whereas perhaps we could have done a lot for those clients if they had come to us a couple of years earlier.

As I keep saying, there are four ways to pay for long-term care. If you can't or don't want to pay out of your own pocket, the best thing to do is plan ahead. Purchase a long-term care insurance policy or plan in advance for Medicaid or veterans' benefits. If you find your family in a situation where advance planning is no longer an option, don't try to figure things out on your own. Understand that you have more options than privately paying the long-term care bill until you run out of money. And while setting up your long-term care plan, don't forget my warning: If you focus exclusively on one strand of planning, you can cause bigger problems than you solve. Don't forget that a good plan keeps your estate out of probate, avoids unnecessary taxation, and addresses your long-term care needs.

Conclusion

In the 1990 comedy *Home Alone*, eight-year-old Kevin McCallister thinks his wish has come true. On the eve of a family trip to Paris, and after a night of ridicule that only younger siblings understand, he wishes that his family will disappear. Through a series of unlikely events that night and the next morning, his family leaves in a rush for their Paris flight without him. He awakes to an empty house, and he is elated.

While wandering around his neighborhood enjoying his newfound freedom, Kevin overhears a couple of con men discussing plans to burglarize his house. As soon as Kevin learns that his house is at risk, he is motivated to do whatever he can to protect it. Kevin sets clever booby traps that the con men encounter upon breaking in. Kevin and his traps force the burglars out, but the men corner Kevin in a nearby vacant house. While the bad guys argue about how to extract their revenge, a neighbor appears unexpectedly and coldcocks the con men with a snow shovel. Kevin learned about a threat, developed a plan to address that threat, and with a little help succeeded in protecting his home.

You and Kevin are more alike than you may realize. Your home is at risk. No, I don't mean that a couple of dim-witted con men have been casing the place. Your home is subject to more serious threats than that. And not only your house is vulnerable. Your bank accounts, retirement accounts, and investments all are at risk.

By now you know the threats I'm talking about. A couple of centuries ago, Benjamin Franklin warned about the two certainties for which everyone must plan—death and taxes. The third threat you must anticipate is the need for long-term care and the high costs associated with it. These three threats are much more dangerous than the burglars Kevin fended off with his traps. Addressing all three threats requires a three-stranded approach to planning.

THE FIRST STRAND OF PLANNING

The first certainty in life is death. Without proper planning, everything you own could wind up in probate court when you die. The high costs, long delays, and total lack of privacy associated with probate court make that outcome unacceptable. Whether your assets wind up in probate or not, those assets (or what's left of them) will eventually end up in the hands of your heirs, where they become subject to a whole new set of risks. If you do not control how your assets pass to your heirs, those assets can be lost to the legal troubles of those you hoped to benefit. Your estate could be sucked into your son's divorce or daughter's bankruptcy. Your disabled child could become ineligible for essential government benefits. Those assets could become a curse for an unprepared or unsophisticated heir. The first strand of planning addresses all these risks.

The first strand ensures that your estate gets where you want it to go in the way you want it to get there, without passing through probate. In most cases, this strand involves the use of a trust as your primary estate-planning tool; the trust acts as a replacement for a last will and testament. Using a trust allows you to direct your estate to your heirs at death without lawyers and judges, with minimal cost and delays. It also allows you to protect your heirs from themselves and others. A trust can protect your heirs from themselves if they are too young to inherit assets outright or are old enough but lack the skills to manage an inheritance. A trust can also protect your heirs from others, such as a future ex-spouse and creditors. The first strand is the foundation of any strong estate plan.

THE SECOND STRAND OF PLANNING

Franklin's second certainty in life—taxes—also demands careful planning. Several common methods people use to keep their estates out of probate court can subject their heirs to unnecessary taxation that could cost them more than probate. One of the simplest ways to keep real estate out of probate, for example, is the quitclaim deed. But as you learned in part 2, transferring property using a quitclaim deed often results in higher capital gains taxes when your heirs eventually sell the property. The same undesirable result stems from the lifetime transfer of stock from parent to child.

The second strand of planning ensures that your heirs do not become subject to unnecessary taxation as a result of your chosen means of transfer. With most assets, you can protect your heirs from capital gains taxes by using a trust instead of lifetime gifts. When you gift property, you also give the recipient your old tax basis. When your heirs sell the property, they have to pay capital gains taxes on the difference between what they sell it for and what you paid for it. On the other hand, if they inherit your property at your death, preferably through a trust to address the concerns of the first strand, they also inherit a stepped-up tax basis. With this method of transfer, the only capital gains tax they pay when they sell the property is on the difference between what they sell it for and the value at your death. That distinction often reduces or eliminates capital gains taxes altogether.

Eliminating capital gains taxes is only one part of the second strand of planning. If you have IRAs and other types of tax-qualified retirement accounts, your method of transfer can also have a huge impact on your heirs' income tax liability. Income taxes are not an issue with most assets you pass on, but without careful planning, your entire IRA could be subjected to immediate taxation upon your death. Using an IRA trust can extend tax deferrals for as long as legally possible while protecting your heirs from themselves and others.

THE THIRD STRAND OF PLANNING

More than two-thirds of adults older than sixty-five will need long-term care at some point, and its high cost can wipe out an estate in no time, making the probable need for long-term care the third threat that demands careful planning. You can have the best plan for avoiding probate and protecting your heirs, and you can maximize every tax advantage available, but if nothing is left because you were forced to spend it all on long-term care in your final years, what have you accomplished?

The third strand of planning ensures you have something left to pass on. The safest bet is to plan ahead. If you don't want to pay for long-term care out of your own pocket, you have only three other options. Each is more readily available—in some cases available only—if you plan well in advance of need.

The first way to cover long-term care costs is long-term care insurance. Medicare, Medicare supplements, and private health insurance won't do it. But you must purchase long-term care insurance when you're healthy enough to make it through medical underwriting. The other two methods available to pay for long-term care costs are veterans' benefits and Medicaid. Because of their strict asset limits and formal (Medicaid) or informal (veterans' benefits) lookback rules, which discourage the transfer of assets near the time of need, both options are more likely to be available to those who plan ahead. But even those who fail to plan ahead for eligibility for these benefits have hope for gaining coverage without spending down everything they have. There are ways to pull a rabbit out of the hat.

Strong plans consider all three strands. Just as a three-stranded rope is stronger than a rope of only one or two strands, a strong estate plan encompasses all three strands of planning. Focusing on only one strand of planning while ignoring the others can have disastrous consequences. What would have happened if Kevin had focused all his attention on one burglar and completely ignored the other? But that's exactly what many planners do. They give all their attention to avoiding probate while ignoring the tax consequences of the plan or the impact it will have on their client's chances of qualifying for long-term care benefits.

Kevin's story teaches us one more thing: Even though he was highly motivated to protect his home once he realized it was at risk, he wasn't able to do it alone. Despite his best efforts, the con men eventually cornered him. To his relief, his neighbor appeared at just the right moment to help him.

The need to plan for several threats all at once makes estate planning complicated. Balancing the three strands of planning can be a challenge. Don't try to do it alone. You need a team of advisers on your side—competent advisers with the right motivations. One member of your team should be a good estate-planning attorney. But remember my grandparents' attorney? I believe he had good motives, but he didn't have a system in place to make sure my grandparents understood and used their trust properly, so it failed. Remember Michael Jackson's estate-planning attorneys? (I'm less certain of their motives, considering the huge fees they've earned on his probate.) Not everyone who is willing to write a trust for you is interested in or capable of helping you to balance all three strands of planning.

If you don't have a good estate-planning attorney and don't know where to find one, a good place to start is the website for the National Elder Law Foundation, www.nelf.org. NELF is accredited by the American Bar Association, and it is the only organization authorized to confer the designation of certified elder law attorney (CELA). More than four hundred CELAs are in practice across the country. Attorneys who have received the CELA designation have demonstrated expertise in the field, passed a tough examination, and must meet the foundation's continuing education requirements to retain that designation.

Your team should also include a dependable financial adviser who can provide guidance to you in the years ahead and to your heirs upon your death, especially if you are passing on assets, such as IRAs, that require some knowledge of the tax code. Another key member of your team should be an accountant who can talk to you about more than just your basic income tax return—someone who can advise you on the best ways to save (or spend) your IRA, who can put your mind at ease about the federal gift tax, and who understands your goals regarding the capital gains tax.

Did you see the look on Kevin's face when he realized that he had protected his family's home? He was proud. He was relieved. He was thrilled. That's how you feel when you have a plan that accomplishes your goals. That's how you feel when you beat procrastination, overcome your fears, think about things you'd prefer not to think about, and take care of business. Ignorance may be bliss, but you can't claim ignorance anymore. You know the threats you face, and you know how to face them. And when you take them on—when you implement your three-stranded plan—you will be relieved. You will have peace of mind. You will be proud that you took action to protect yourself, your family, and your estate.

For Easy
Reference

A Quick Look at Basic Medicaid Rules

Medicaid rules vary from state to state; this summary outlines the basic rules for qualification that apply in most states in most circumstances. Generally, to qualify for Medicaid, an applicant in need of long-term care services must meet both an income test (except in states that have abolished the income limit) and an asset test. The applicant must also disclose all transfers of assets occurring in the five years preceding submission of the application, a period referred to as the five-year lookback. Applicants are subject to a gifting penalty for nonexempt transfers made during the five-year lookback.

Those covered by Medicaid must contribute the majority of their income to the cost of long-term care each month—a copay toward the cost of care—after permissible deductions for health insurance and drug plan premiums and a small personal needs allowance. The copay is called the patient liability. Medicaid covers the rest of the facility's charges.

THE INCOME TEST

In states that have an income limit, that state will publish the limit in its Medicaid regulations, and the limit usually increases each year. The income limit in most states is about $2,200 per month. When a Medicaid applicant is married, only the income of the spouse applying for coverage counts under the income test. The income of the spouse not filing for Medicaid is protected. When determining qualification under the income test, Medicaid uses gross income figures before any deductions for taxes or insurance premiums, not net income.

For those with monthly income higher than the limit, Medicaid allows the use of an irrevocable income trust, more commonly called a Miller trust, to avoid disqualification. At its core, the Miller trust is a trust checking account through which most of the Medicaid applicant's income is funneled to the nursing home every month.

When the spouse still living at home does not receive a certain minimum level of income to meet expenses (as determined by each state each year), the independent spouse can retain a portion of the Medicaid applicant's income before payment to the facility of the patient liability so that the independent spouse's income rises to the minimum level set by the state.

THE ASSET TEST

Medicaid allows single applicants only a few permissible assets—a house, a vehicle, and a prepaid burial plan. Aside from those limited assets, an applicant can have no more than $2,000, whether that is the value of a second vehicle, the cash value of a life insurance policy, or funds in financial accounts. Although the house is a permissible asset, most states engage in estate recovery at the death of the Medicaid recipient. This allows the state to put a lien against the house, if it is still in the name of the Medicaid recipient at the time of death, and makes home ownership by a single Medicaid recipient inadvisable in most circumstances.

Medicaid rules are more flexible for married applicants. In addition to the permissible assets allowed to single applicants, the spouse of a married applicant can keep one-half of the couple's assets as of the date of entry into a long-term care facility but limited to certain minimum and maximum levels determined by the state each year. In many states, the spouse of a married Medicaid applicant will be allowed to keep at least $25,000 in assets but no more than about $120,000 under this rule.

GIFTING RULES

Because Medicaid has such strict asset limits, it imposes and enforces strict gifting rules to prevent applicants from attempting to meet Medicaid's asset test by transferring assets just before they apply.

Medicaid has a five-year lookback, which is a window in time before application through which the state is permitted to look for asset transfers and then penalize the applicant for any it finds. In other words, when an applicant for Medicaid submits an application, that applicant must also submit a statement disclosing all asset transfers that occurred in the five years before the date of application.

Gifts or transfers during the five-year lookback do not always mean that the applicant will be ineligible for Medicaid for the next five years or even that coverage will be denied until the five-year anniversary of the disclosed gifts. Rather, if an applicant for Medicaid made gifts or transferred assets for less than fair market value during the five years previous to applying, Medicaid will impose a penalty period during which the applicant must wait for Medicaid coverage after moving to a long-term care facility and meeting all other requirements for Medicaid coverage.

Certain transfers are exempt from the gifting penalty, but those exceptions vary from state to state. One common exemption protects the transfer of assets between spouses. Another exempts the transfer of assets to a disabled child. In many states, Medicaid will reduce or eliminate a gifting penalty if the recipient of the transferred assets returns some or all of those assets to the applicant.

A Quick Look at Basic VA Aid and Attendance Rules

This summary outlines the basic rules applicable in most circumstances for qualifying for the VA Pension with Aid and Attendance. Generally a claimant must meet three separate sets of criteria. The claimant must be a veteran with qualifying military service or the surviving spouse of such a veteran, have qualifying health needs, and meet financial tests imposed by the VA.

The aid and attendance benefit pays a nontaxable pension benefit to qualified claimants by direct deposit to the claimant's account, much like social security. The amount varies according to the marital status of the applicant, with surviving spouses receiving the lowest benefit amount (about $1,150 per month) and married veterans receiving the highest (about $2,100 per month). Award amounts typically increase each year with inflation.

MILITARY SERVICE

The benefit is available only to veterans and the surviving spouses of veterans who served on active duty during a congressionally declared period of war. Qualifying periods of war include World War II, the Vietnam War, the Korean War, and the Persian Gulf War. Claimants must submit discharge papers proving service on active duty for at least ninety days, any one day of which corresponded to a period of formally declared war. The discharge must be of any type other than dishonorable. Surviving spouses seeking the benefit must also provide proof of marriage to the veteran and a copy of the veteran's death certificate.

HEALTH NEEDS

The aid and attendance benefit is available only to claimants who have health needs that require long-term care assistance. Those who are legally blind or who reside in a nursing home automatically meet this requirement. Claimants with a diagnosis of dementia usually meet this requirement as well. In all other cases, claimants must submit a physician's affidavit, completed by a doctor chosen by the claimant, to establish the need for assistance with at least two activities of daily living.

The long-term care services may be provided by a facility or in the home. The VA does not require that providers of in-home care have any special certification or training. In fact, family members of the claimant may provide the care. A reduced VA pension may be awarded to veterans older than sixty-five who meet all other requirements but do not require long-term care.

FINANCIAL REQUIREMENTS

The VA uses both a fairly complex income test and an asset test in determining qualification for the aid and attendance benefit.

The VA's formula determines a claimant's "income for VA purposes" (IVAP). The IVAP compares the claimant's gross income from all sources to the claimant's qualified recurring medical expenses. If a claimant's income is less than or equal to the qualified recurring medical expenses reported, that claimant qualifies for the maximum aid and attendance benefit available based on the claimant's marital status. If the claimant's income is greater than the qualified recurring medical expenses, the claimant may still receive the aid and attendance benefit, but the VA will reduce the maximum award by that claimant's IVAP. The VA will deny benefits to claimants with an IVAP that is equal to or greater than the maximum award amount for which they applied. When a claimant is married, the VA income test considers the gross income and the qualified recurring medical expenses of both spouses.

Qualified recurring medical expenses include health insurance and drug plan premiums, premiums paid for long-term care insurance, costs incurred for home caregiver assistance, and fees paid to long-term care facilities, including assisted living facilities and nursing homes. It is not necessary that the claimant have paid these expenses before applying, but to meet the income test, the claimant must begin paying them by the time of application at the latest.

The VA excludes certain assets from the asset test. Claimants need not report their house or vehicle to the VA, but all other assets will factor into the VA's analysis. While the VA does not publish a rule setting the maximum asset level permissible, the department denies married claimants with countable assets valued at more than $80,000. Many attorneys advise single claimants to file for this benefit only if their countable assets are worth less than $40,000.

Current law includes no formal lookback period for transfers of assets before application. Accordingly, the VA cannot assign a penalty period for asset transfers, no matter when they occur in relation to the date of application. However, the VA does use its power to compare the information reported on a claimant's application against information reported to the IRS under the claimant's social security number, and the VA demands a detailed explanation for any discrepancies. This means that when the income and assets reported on an application do not match the information reported to the IRS in previous years, the VA may challenge and delay the application despite the absence of a formal lookback rule.

Claimants should also be aware that the VA has proposed major rule changes that would impose a three-year lookback. This lookback would be a window in time before application through which the VA could look for and then penalize asset transfers. It is not clear when or if those rule changes will take effect, but potential claimants with assets that exceed the limit for the aid and attendance benefit should be aware of the informal lookback currently applied by the VA, as well as the possibility that a formal lookback will be imposed for all asset transfers.

Acknowledgments

———

This book would not exist without the patience and support of my wife, Kim. My children helped, too, although they may not realize it. My son, J. Dawson, spent many nights by my side reading his school books while I wrote. I appreciated his company, even though I know his primary motivation was delaying going to bed. And my daughter, Ali, had a knack for reminding me when I needed it the most that the reason I was writing this book—and the reason we plan—is to take care of the people we love.

My grandparents, Elbert and Florene Elrod, and their three children inspired me to write this book by admirably tackling everything life threw at them in the best way they knew how. They were a great example of how a family is supposed to work. My hope is that through this book, their story will help other families avoid some of the problems they faced. I owe special thanks to my parents, Jimmy and Kathy Elrod, for bringing life to my grandparents' story by providing many of the background details I forgot or never knew.

Three good friends deserve recognition as well for reviewing and providing valuable comments on this book. My law partner, Bethany Pike, took the lead on part one, my accountant, Jordan Woolbright, cleaned up part two, and my case manager, Amy Cook, assisted on part three.

Finally, I want to thank my editor, Polly Kummel, who put tremendous effort into this book and kept me in line every step of the way.

About the Author

JUSTIN ELROD is the founder of The Elrod Firm, an Estate Planning and Elder Law practice. He is one of only three Certified Elder Law Attorneys in Arkansas, and he sits on the board of directors of the National Elder Law Foundation. Elrod is an accredited attorney with the Department of Veteran Affairs, and he regularly speaks to groups across the state on the areas of estate planning, asset protection planning, and long-term care benefits. He lives in Arkansas with his wife and two children.